In treating symptoms (sexual or otherwise) we are missing the existential big picture and Dan's book is not just a tonic to the dessicated solutions-oriented ethos we have all internalized, it is a manifesto and rallying cry and to live authentically, work deeply and create meaning.

Ian Kerner, sex therapist and best-selling author of *She Comes First*

Written in a lively, empathic, and often witty style, mercifully free from psychobabble, this book is intended for clinicians and male patients, but will also be of interest to many others. One feels pleasure from reading the book, never Schadenfreude. If the penis could read, it would surely learn much from this wise and compassionate study.

Jeffrey Berman, distinguished teaching professor, Department of English, University of Albany, author of *Writing the Talking Cure: Irvin D. Yalom and the Literature of Psychotherapy*

Weaving together patient stories with literature and philosophy, this compelling and compassionate book challenges us to look beyond moral judgments to find meaning and joy in the sexual lives of our patients.

Kathryn Hall, editor, *Principles and Practice of Sex Therapy*, 6th edition, book review editor, *Journal of Sex and Marital Therapy*

This is not a lengthy philosophical tome on death anxiety; it is a satisfying and nourishing journey. Reading Dr. Watter's book will significantly transform your clinical perspective leading to more sophisticated ways of helping men with their sexual struggles and relationships.

Stanley E. Althof, executive director, Center for Marital and Sexual Health of South Florida, professor emeritus, Case Western Reserve University School of Medicine

The meaning of sexual disorder and its resolution are often, as, if not more important than accomplishing the behavioral change first sought by the patient. Watter challenges the reader to engage that dialectic in an accessible manner. It is a pleasure to recommend this book for every sex therapist's library.

Michael A. Perelman, co-director, Human Sexuality Program, clinical professor emeritus of Psychology in Psychiatry

THE EXISTENTIAL IMPORTANCE OF THE PENIS

The first of its kind, this book applies existential principles to sexual problems, providing clinicians with the tools to understand male sexuality more deeply.

Alighting from the existential psychotherapy tenets of Irvin D. Yalom, Watter introduces the notion that the penis is a conduit for male emotion and hence regulates men's ability to form and experience intimate relationships. Subsequent chapters explore an existential view of male sexual dysfunction, nonsexual trauma, hypersexuality, changing bodies through illness, age, and injury, and examines badly behaved men to understand the meaning of certain behaviors.

This book will be an invaluable resource for sex therapists, marriage and family therapists, psychologists, and social workers in practice and in training, assisting them to develop the therapeutic skills that will improve their understanding of men's psychological experience.

Daniel N. Watter has been a practicing clinical and forensic psychologist and certified sex therapist for more than 35 years. He is the past president of the Society for Sex Therapy and Research.

THE EXISTENTIAL IMPORTANCE OF THE PENIS

A Guide to Understanding Male Sexuality

Daniel N. Watter

Routledge
Taylor & Francis Group

NEW YORK AND LONDON

Cover image: gremlin; Getty Images

First published 2023
by Routledge
605 Third Avenue, New York, NY 10158

and by Routledge
4 Park Square, Milton Park, Abingdon, Oxon, OX14 4RN

Routledge is an imprint of the Taylor & Francis Group, an informa business

© 2023 Daniel N. Watter

Library of Congress Cataloging-in-Publication Data
Names: Watter, Daniel, author.
Title: The existential importance of the penis : a guide to understanding male
    sexuality / Daniel N. Watter.
Description: New York, NY : Routledge, 2023. | Includes bibliographical references
    and index.
Identifiers: LCCN 2022018145 (print) | LCCN 2022018146 (ebook) | ISBN
    9780367635084 (hbk) | ISBN 9780367651114 (pbk) | ISBN 9781003127871 (ebk)
Subjects: LCSH: Men—Sexual behavior. | Penis—Social aspects. | Sexual disorders. |
    Sex (Psychology)
Classification: LCC HQ28 .W38 2023 (print) | LCC HQ28 (ebook) |
    DDC 306.70811—dc23/eng/20220606
LC record available at https://lccn.loc.gov/2022018145
LC ebook record available at https://lccn.loc.gov/2022018146

ISBN: 978-0-367-63508-4 (hbk)
ISBN: 978-0-367-65111-4 (pbk)
ISBN: 978-1-003-12787-1 (ebk)

DOI: 10.4324/9781003127871

Typeset in Joanna
by Apex CoVantage, LLC

To my inspiring, generous mentor, Irvin D. Yalom, M.D., whose words ripple throughout this book.

To the memory of my sweet, wonderful mother, Dorothy H. Watter, whose words ripple throughout me.

And

To my beloved son, Michael Steven Watter, and grandson, Jayden Jacob Watter, in the hope that my words ripple through them as they navigate their paths through manhood.

CONTENTS

ACKNOWLEDGMENTS

There are so many people to thank for helping to make this book a reality. First and foremost is the brilliant psychiatrist Irvin D. Yalom, M.D., for his pioneering work in existential psychotherapy. Irv has been a great mentor and supporter of my work. He has been encouraging from the beginning, reading through draft chapters, making suggestions, and providing needed affirmation that I was onto something of importance. Now in his 90s, Irv continues to write and consult, and his words will ripple through generations to come.

I have been very fortunate to have had the opportunity to work with and learn from so many lovely patients. This book represents you and your stories. I hope I have done you and your stories justice. I have made every effort to conceal identities and create case studies that are more amalgams of clinical narratives than anyone's actual story. However, if you think you recognize yourself in any of my case studies, please know that I have been honored to work with you, and you have taught me much. Also know that since these are case amalgams, seeing yourself lets you know that you are not alone in your suffering. Many men have struggled with similar issues, both sexual and existential, and though we don't often discuss them with others, we are brothers in living. Thank you for allowing me to journey alongside you.

The folks at Routledge deserve special mention for allowing this book to come to fruition. Heather Evans and Georgina Clutterbuck have been most helpful and encouraging as editors, and their guidance has been invaluable.

Helen Robin has been particularly helpful in providing access to Woody Allen and making helpful edits and corrections to the scripts of some of his films.

Loudon Wainwright III was also very responsive and accommodating in clarifying, editing, and providing context in order for me to more deeply understand his writings and songs.

I have been fortunate to have a strong, loving professional community to lean on. Several friends and colleagues at the Society for Sex Therapy and Research (SSTAR) have been instrumental in guiding my career. Some are no longer with us, such as Drs. Peter Fagan and Sandra Leiblum, both of whom were great mentors in my early years. Thanks also to Dr. Michael Perelman, who gave me some of my first opportunities to write for a professional audience, Dr. Marta Meana, who set the path for me to follow, to Dr. Peggy Kleinplatz for teaching me so much about the importance of questioning the status quo, and to Dr. Kathryn Hall for being about the best friend anyone could have. Kathryn has been a huge supporter of this project. She read every page, gave insightful and detailed edits, and challenged me to think more carefully and dig deeper to find my own voice. Thank you, Kathryn. Your friendship means the world to me. Everyone should be fortunate enough to have a friend like you.

Jeffrey Berman, Ph.D., deserves a special kind of thanks. I first learned of him by reading his wonderful book, *Writing the Talking Cure: Irvin D. Yalom and the Literature of Psychotherapy*. I enjoyed the book so much that I soon read all of Jeff's other texts. He is a superb writer with a vast knowledge of psychology and the psychotherapy process. He, too, read every page of this manuscript, made helpful edits, recommended several valuable sources, used his academic credentials to assist me in obtaining hard-to-find articles, and generously agreed to write the Foreword to this book. I consider Jeff a valued teacher, mentor, and friend. Over the past few years, we have developed a warm, dear friendship. Oh, by the way, did I tell you we've never met? As a matter of fact, I've never even heard his voice! All our conversations have been via email. Jeff is truly an amazing and giving person. His being so generous with his wisdom and his time to a stranger has taught me a great deal about the importance of offering oneself selflessly, relationally, and munificently. Jeff is a prince, and I hope to do for others what he has done for me. His students are fortunate, indeed (I really wanted to say, "his students are *very* fortunate, indeed," but Jeff keeps reminding me to limit my use of the word "very"!).

I have also had the rarest kind of kismet in my relational life. I was raised by marvelous parents and found the love of my life, Laurie, who has taught me the many benefits of living a relationally connected life. Laurie and I met as young teens and have now been married for 44 years. We have two outstanding children and one absolutely delightful grandson. I am a lucky man.

The penis speaks. Listen to it. It has much to say.

CREDITS LIST

FOREWORD

Phallocentric thinking, an ideology in which the phallus, or male sexual member, symbolizes male dominance, is a pejorative expression in psychology, literature, philosophy, linguistics, medicine, and healthcare. Phallocentric thinking, which can be defined wryly as "thinking with the wrong head," represents patriarchal culture at its worst. For this reason, the title of Dr. Daniel N. Watter's book, *The Existential Importance of the Penis: A Guide to Understanding Male Sexuality*, is startling. Yet it is also an accurate and brave title, one that represents a new way of thinking about male sexual problems.

"What does a woman want?" Freud asked famously, or infamously, suggesting that female sexuality represents, psychologically, a dark continent. Dr. Watter asks, "What does a man want?"—particularly a man with erectile difficulties. There are many theoretical approaches to erection/orgasm/ejaculation/desire conflicts, but this book is unique in offering an existential understanding of the penis as a life force, an antidote to death anxiety. An existential model involves treating the whole person, not simply a man's sexual equipment. "The task of therapy," Dr. Watter writes, "is to help the man decipher what the penis is saying to him." In the author's view, the penis symbolizes male desire and male vulnerability, including the fear of exposure and nakedness. Rejecting diagnostic labels as inherently reductive, he shows how sexual dysfunction frequently reveals the existential terror of dying and death. He also demonstrates persuasively how male sexual dysfunction is often caused by the memory of an earlier trauma.

Throughout the book, Dr. Watter uses case study material and clinical vignettes sensitively and effectively: he is a gifted storyteller. Additionally, he draws upon literature and philosophy to strengthen his argument. He recognizes that novelists and philosophers have profound insight into the human condition, thus representing an invaluable resource for psychotherapists. His discussion of the sexual conflicts of Tony Soprano in the popular HBO series The Sopranos, Jake Barnes in Hemingway's The Sun Also Rises, and Alex Portnoy in Philip Roth's celebrated novel Portnoy's Complaint adds a fascinating literary dimension to the book.

One of the dedicatees of The Existential Importance of the Penis is Irvin D. Yalom, America's most influential living psychiatrist and, next to Freud, the greatest writer of psychotherapy tales. Yalom has served as an inspirational mentor to Daniel N. Watter and to me, I should add, in my approach to literature. Yalom's signature ideas—the centrality of the therapeutic relationship, therapist transparency, here-and-now therapy, "rippling" (the effect we have on other people and, in turn, their effect on others), and the prevalence of death anxiety—have indelibly shaped Dr. Watter's thinking. One repays a teacher badly if one remains only a student, Nietzsche said provocatively; Dr. Watter has taken this lesson to heart, pointing out how Yalom's work can be extended to the treatment of male sexual problems.

Written in a lively, conversational, empathic, and often witty style, mercifully free from psychobabble, The Existential Importance of the Penis is intended mainly for clinicians and male patients, but it will also be of interest to many others, including aging men who experience a "quiet" penis. Female readers and nonpatients will also profit from reading the book. Dr. Watter offers us an intriguing guide to "penis speak." One feels pleasure from reading the book, never Schadenfreude. If the penis could read, it would surely learn much from this wise and compassionate study.

Jeffrey Berman
Distinguished Teaching Professor,
Department of English, Humanities Building, Room 348,
Albany, New York 12222, (518) 442–4084,
jberman@albany.edu

IN THE BEGINNING . . .

My mother was a great storyteller. One of her favorite tales recalled a time when I was very young, and she was giving me a bath. After washing my genitalia, she remembers me requesting her to "Wash it again, mommy." This was a moment of great significance for us both. For me, at this youthful age, I had my first conscious indication of the importance of my penis. For my mother, she had her first conscious indication that it was time for me to start taking my own baths.

INTRODUCTION

This is not a book about how the penis works. This is also not a book about how to be a better lover or have better sex. For those interested in those subjects, there is a plethora of books devoted to those topics. This is a book about the psychological lives of men. The *existential* psychological lives of men, and how much of the psychological concerns of men are communicated through the functioning, or lack thereof, of their penis.

I have been a practicing psychologist and sex therapist for more than 35 years. During that time, I have sat with hundreds and hundreds of men who have agonized over the compromised functioning of their penis. Some have a penis that no longer functions as desired due to physical limitations such as age, injury, or illness, while others have unwanted changes in penile functioning for more psychological or relational reasons. Whatever the cause, these men often express great angst when their penis ceases to become erect or stay erect during a sexual encounter with a partner. Men with erectile difficulties have told me that they feel "broken," "less of a man," "weak," and "inadequate." They describe feelings of humiliation, shame, embarrassment, vulnerability,

DOI: 10.4324/9781003127871-1

and losses of self-esteem, self-worth, and self-efficacy. Urologists will confirm that historically, men have gone to great pains (often literally) to restore penile functioning to its desired level. Vacuum pumps, penile implants, urethral suppositories, and injections directly into the penis are all highly sought interventions that men will endure in the quest to restore penile function. More recently, oral medications have become the first line of medical treatment, and while removing much of the physical discomfort of the more invasive methods, they don't necessarily reduce the psychological unease.

Many who have written about male sexuality in the past have largely focused on the disappointment these men feel because they are unable to have sex. Certainly, that is a significant aspect to their suffering. However, to assume that the inability to have sex only for the sake of *sexual pleasure*, not to mention to undergo the invasive, uncomfortable, and often frustrating medical interventions, would likely miss the deeper significance of reduced penile functioning.

My training in sex therapy was much like that of most of my colleagues. The field of sex therapy was popularized by William Masters and Virginia Johnson in the early 1970s (Masters & Johnson, 1970). Most of us in my generation were trained in the Masters and Johnson sex therapy protocols and later influenced by the rise of cognitive-behavioral therapy (CBT). We focused on behavioral interventions that were designed to reduce sexual performance anxiety and improve couples' communication. I practiced this way, happily, for many years before becoming somewhat concerned that I wasn't helping my patients get deep enough into their psyches to genuinely improve their lives. Sure, sex was often better, but an underlying unhappiness and lack of life satisfaction were still present.

It was then that I first became acquainted with the work of Stanford University psychiatrist Irvin D. Yalom, M.D., and his work in existential psychotherapy. Actually, that's not quite true. My introduction to Yalom was as a young graduate student taking a class in group therapy. The text used for that class was Yalom's *The Theory and Practice of Group Therapy*. This text, now about to be released in its sixth edition (Yalom & Leszcz, 2020), was even then considered a classic in the group therapy world. I studied the book, learned from it, but frankly missed the most important features—namely the importance of an existential lens in the psychotherapy process. I was young, naïve, and likely hadn't experienced enough of life and the world for Yalom's words to resonate with me. However, about 25 years ago, I came upon Yalom's first book of psychotherapy tales, Love's Executioner and Other Tales of Psychotherapy (Yalom, 1989), and my way of thinking about problems of the human condition, including sexual function, was transformed. Yalom's work introduced me to the process of looking for the meaning behind the presenting symptom and to consider how the presenting symptom may be a representation of the existentially based conflicts my patients were struggling to navigate. Existential therapy (which will be described in detail in a later chapter) focuses on the meaning and protection of one's existence and thus provides a much deeper examination of the complaints people present in psychotherapy. Why is this man having erection/orgasm/ejaculation/ desire problems? Why is this man suffering so because as a result of his radical prostatectomy to eradicate his prostate cancer, he can no longer achieve satisfactory penile erection? What is the meaning of these events to these men who now feel so woefully inadequate as men? As a young man, these questions never entered my awareness.

This was not the first time my youth and limited life experience presented in my practice of sex therapy. When I was just starting out in practice, I was asked to speak at a meeting of my local hospital's Impotents Anonymous chapter. Impotents Anonymous (IA) was an organization that was founded by husband and wife Bruce and Eileen MacKenzie. The MacKenzies had been married for several years and struggled with 58-year-old Bruce's erectile problems. The MacKenzie's did not know where to turn, and both the medical and psychological communities had few practitioners who were well educated in sexual matters. Taking their lead from Alcoholics Anonymous (AA), the MacKenzie's determined to develop a support group for men with erectile difficulties and their partners. The organization grew rapidly, and for several years, there were chapters throughout the United States. Most of the chapters had a urologist as their organizer and medical consultant, but in the early 1980s, there were few medical options available for the treatment of men's sexual problems. This was before the days of oral medications such as sildenafil citrate (Viagra) and before the advent of penile injections. Medicine was primarily giving men testosterone, herbs such as yohimbine, vacuum pumps to draw blood into the penis, and surgical penile implants. Very few urologists were comfortable addressing the psychological and relational issues of erectile dysfunction, and so I was asked to do a presentation on helping men and their partners stay sexually active and connected despite the man's inability to achieve or maintain an erection.

The prevailing narrative of the day was that erections are not necessary for enjoyable sex and that men should stop focusing on their penis to be less "goal oriented" and performance focused (Zilbergeld, 1978). While this is certainly good counsel, and good sex certainly goes well beyond erectile capability, it was a difficult sell to the men whose penises were not responsive in the ways they wanted them to be. So, here I am, all of 26 years old, a newly minted "doctor" and I am going to tell this audience of mostly 50-plus-year-olds how to have sex. Even as I write this today, I cringe from my audacity, arrogance, and naïveté. Nevertheless, I begin my talk to a very receptive, respectful audience of about 100 people. I then decide the time is right to make my essential point that sex does not have to include hard penises and intercourse to be satisfying. This is a revelation that I'm sure will absolutely transform their sexual sorrows into renewed hope and excitement. I ask a man in the front row if I may use him as a foil. He genially agreed, and I asked him:

"Sir, what is your favorite meal?" "Filet mignon," he replied. "Great," says I. "And what is your second-favorite meal?" He thinks a bit and says, "Chicken parmigiana." "Excellent," I said. I continued with, "So, let's assume that you go to your favorite restaurant and the server asks what you would like for dinner. You reply, with excitement, that you would like some of the chef's wonderful filet mignon. The server apologizes and tells you that they are all out of filet mignon that evening, but the chef has prepared a delicious chicken parmigiana. Would you then get up and storm out of the restaurant because you were so disappointed?" He looked at me carefully and said, "No, I would not. I would go with the chicken parmigiana." "And would you enjoy it?" I inquired. To which he responded, "Yes, I would probably enjoy it very much." Having made my point in a most showman-like fashion, I said, "So, you see. Even though you couldn't have your first choice and had to settle for your second choice, you were still very happy and walked away quite satisfied." I then began to parade around the front of the room to continue my talk and gloat in proving my point that even though intercourse may be what is most desired, nonpenetrative sex can also be extremely satisfying, when I hear: "Excuse me." I turn back to my front-row foil, and he is standing looking at me with a pained look on his face. "But if I was being told I could never have filet mignon again . . ." Guess who had a transformative educational experience that day!

Even with my obvious youth and inexperience, I could tell that I was seeing more than I understood about these men and their sexual troubles that evening. Still, it was several years before I had a clue as to what it was.

Why I Wrote This Book

As the years went by, I became increasingly aware of the depth of the suffering of the men I was treating. I knew that the functioning of their penises meant much more to them than just the ability to have sex. My work in existential therapy provided me with many new insights and ideas that I was able to use very effectively with my patients. But it wasn't until I came across a New York Times news report in the January 13, 2017, edition titled "Study Maps 'Uniquely Devastating' Genital Injuries Among Troops" (Grady, 2017) that the true depth of men's distress became clear to me. Reporter Grady reported on an article from the Journal of Urology that revealed that from the period of 2001–2013, 1,367 men in the United States military suffered genital injuries, mostly from bomb blasts, while serving in Iraq or Afghanistan. Most of the wounded men (approximately 94%) were 35 years old or younger. Grady further reported that the loss of genital functioning left these men at a particularly high risk for suicide.

I found this article to be particularly moving and knew these men would have trouble adjusting and coping. However, it wasn't until Grady's (2018) follow-up article, "'Whole Again': A Vet Maimed by an I.E.D. Receives a Transplanted Penis," and another article by Antonia Noori Farzan (2019) in the Washington Post titled "A Veteran Wounded by an IED is 'Feeling Whole' Now after a Breakthrough Penis and Scrotum Transplant" that the true significance of these injuries struck me. Doctors at the Johns Hopkins University Hospital had just performed the first penis transplant on an injured veteran. This was only the third operation of this sort ever done and the first done due to a combat injury. Prior to a transplant, doctors were able to create an artificial phallus, but patients would require a penile implant to have an erection and be able to have penetrative sex. Now, however, with the potential of a transplant, a man could, perhaps, have a naturally functioning penis. The operation, which is still in its infancy, takes approximately 14 hours of surgery. At a cost of $300,000 to $400,000, this option would be out of reach for many. But as fascinating as this development was, the greater revelation was yet to come.

Grady and Farzan reported on interviews with the man (who asked to use the pseudonym "Ray") who had undergone the penis transplant. He reported that after his injury, he was unable to view himself as a man. He believed his life was essentially over and contemplated suicide. The doctors had told him that his injuries were irreparable and permanent. During his time in the military hospital, he felt lonely, embarrassed, and full of shame. He, much like Hemingway's Jake Barnes, observed that male soldiers often chide that after surviving an explosion, they would check their genitals first. One of his colleagues in a neighboring bed said (not knowing what Ray's injuries were) that if he lost his penis, he would kill himself. As the interview continues, it was revealed that Ray had also lost both of his legs in the explosion. His comments about the loss of his legs were particularly striking. Ray said he was able to fairly easily adjust to the loss of his legs and using prostheses but was unable to come to terms with the loss of his penis. He said he would rather have lost limbs, eyesight, hearing, or his life than the use of his penis. These sentiments were also echoed by other male vets after severe genital injury. Following the transplant, he said, "I feel whole again." Grady quotes the chair of plastic and reconstructive surgery at Johns Hopkins, Dr. W.P. Andrew Lee, as saying that goal of this type of transplant is, "to restore a person's sense of identity and manhood." Note that Dr. Lee did not say to restore *sexual ability*. Identity and manhood. Very powerful words indeed. It was now clearer to me than ever before that a man's loss of penile functioning was of a significance that extended far beyond the ability to have penetrative sex. There was something much deeper occurring here, and sex therapy has traditionally not attended to these matters of deep existential despair. This sentiment has been echoed by Courtois and Gerard (2020) regarding their work with men with spinal cord injuries (SCI). They report that the inability to have sexual intercourse is the most common reason for referral in SCI patients. Much of their clinical work is helping men with SCI navigate the existential torment associated with the loss of a fully functioning penis.

Approximately a year ago, I received a letter from a man who had heard me speak on a radio program about the existential despair men with penile injuries endure. He wrote me the following words, and I repeat them here with his permission:

> Hello Dr. Watter. My name is David, and I am a 51-year-old man from Ohio. I heard your interview yesterday on the radio and wanted to reach out. I myself suffered a traumatic injury to my penis, losing the complete head and some of the shaft. This happened to me when I was 11 years old.
>
> I didn't really understand the gravity of my injuries at that age. To their credit, the doctors did about as good a job as possible, though my penis is still horrible to look at. I had lots of difficulty fitting in to social groups afterwards. I gave up most of the things I loved. I gave up baseball and other organized sports, even though I was one of the best athletes on my teams. I did this because I couldn't bring myself to shower with the other guys after the games. I was too embarrassed.
>
> I eventually met my wife and had two children with her, though she, like all the other women I dated left me. As soon as a guy who had a normal looking penis entered their lives, I was either dumped, cheated on, and on occasion publicly humiliated.
>
> My kids are now adults. I've never told them what happened to me, but they can see how utterly destroyed I am. It's truly got nothing to do with sex! It's about feeling normal. It's about having no place in society that you feel you belong. That leaves you incredibly lonely. There are days where I actually go outside, maybe ride my bike or go for a walk. If I didn't have my kids, I would have stepped in front of a bus long ago.
>
> I'm seeing a psychiatrist. But all they do is prescribe me medicine for my depression. And yes, I am very depressed, but it is not the result of any chemical imbalance. It's directly related to how I see myself as a man. I don't believe there's a medicine that can fix that.
>
> After listening to you speak, I can tell you that you speak the truth. The feelings of being broken. That is dead accurate. I feel so broken that I literally push people away from me because I think they can do better.
>
> My life's been really hard. I gave up everything I ever wanted just to be alone so nobody would know about this. I was unsuccessful at that. I've tried hundreds of times to meet someone. Even gave bisexuality a try in the hopes that I could fit in there. However, men are even more hung up on it than women. No guy was interested in me.

I can tell you for absolute certainty that sometime within the next 5 years, once my kids are fully established in their adult lives, I'll probably take my own life.

After so many years of living like this, I've reached the limit of my tolerance. I truly don't want to take my own life. I would much rather just feel normal. I could enjoy everything else if I could just feel that.

Thank you, again, for your words. At least I feel less alone now.

Regards,

Dave

Dave's letter is heartbreaking. This book is for Dave and the countless number of men who share his pain and existential despair.

The Changing Face of Sex Therapy

I was also prompted to write this book as I have noticed that sex therapy seems ripe for change and innovation. For quite some time, the field of sex therapy has stagnated. There has been little growth and a strong resistance to bringing sex therapy into the fold of general psychotherapy (this will be explored in greater detail in Chapter 4). In recent years, this trend seems to have changed. There are now books and book chapters on treating sexual problems utilizing systemic therapy (Weeks et al., 2016), couples therapy (Betchen & Davidson, 2018), narrative therapy (Findlay, 2017; Iasenza, 2020), experiential therapy (Kleinplatz, 2017), mindfulness (Brotto, 2018), imago therapy (Nelson, 2020), and emotionally focused therapy (Johnson, 2017) to name but a few. Sex therapy is maturing and evolving and is opening up to examining and considering new and innovative approaches to treating sexual problems. Therefore, the field seems open to new conceptualizations of sexuality and its conflicts, and the emerging existential sex therapy approach is likely to find acceptance and a home.

The Organization of This Book

This book is essentially organized in two parts. Part One focuses on the theoretical bases of the existential psychotherapy approach to sex therapy. We will begin looking at how the penis "speaks." Chapter 1 will examine the central notion that the penis is the primary conduit for male emotion and thus regulates the closeness/distance that men will be able to experience in intimate relationships. As such, the penis often provides important yet unconscious messages to the man that proceeding sexually is somehow dangerous and inadvisable. Often, such cautions are the result of a triggering of early childhood trauma and are attempts to protect the man from the trauma of further loss, abandonment, or engulfment/suffocation. Many authors have previously examined the effects of *sexual* trauma on male sexuality, but few have carefully considered the impact of nonsexual traumas such as early loss of parents due to death, illness, psychiatric disability, and other adverse childhood experiences. Many of these nonsexual traumas from early relational experiences can be triggered in adulthood and negatively impact male sexual function. In other words, the penis is signaling to the man a potential threat to his *existence*.

Chapter 2 will provide an overview of Yalom's approach to existential psychotherapy. Examined will be an exploration of three of the four central existential conflicts Yalom believes patients bring to psychotherapy, namely freedom, isolation, and meaning.

Chapter 3 will focus on death and the terror of death. Given the centrality of death to all of our existence, this existential given merits a chapter of its own.

Chapter 4 will build on the foundational pieces of existential psychotherapy presented in Chapters 2 and 3 and propose that these principles inform a new approach to the understanding and treatment of male sexual problems known as existential sex therapy.

Part Two will focus on some specific clinical phenomena that have been historically difficult for sex therapy to successfully treat. Chapter 5 will explore the phenomenon of hypersexuality (often referred to as sexual addiction) and how this may be related to the advent of an existential crisis, particularly the terror of death.

Chapter 6 will examine the troublesome sexual behavior of men that is often considered outside the bounds of what is acceptable in our society. Sexual offenses, sexual assaults, and other issues highlighted by the current #Me Too movement will be examined and understood through the lens of existential trauma.

Chapter 7 will deal with issues related to the challenges of dealing with changing bodies due to loss of male agency. Sexual changes because of aging, illness, and injury will be examined and considered. Finally, Chapter 8 will pull it all together and posit suggestions for moving forward in a way that is both effective and deeply helpful to men and their partners.

This book contains many case examples and clinical vignettes. While all of them are based on an amalgam of actual men I've treated, identifying details have been altered to protect their confidentiality.

Intended Audience

This book has been written primarily for those working with men experiencing sexual conflicts and difficulties: sex therapists, psychologists, psychiatrists, social workers, marriage and family therapists, urologists, sexual medicine specialists, and other counselors and physicians wanting to assist men through their times of despair. But I also hope that this book will appeal to men who are not clinicians. I hope that men who are struggling to understand themselves, as well as the messages their penis may be sending them, will also benefit from this book. The ideas presented in this book will provide men, many for the first time, with an explanation and deeper understanding of their internal worlds and the problems and conundrums they are struggling with. For many of these men, bringing their unconscious traumas and conflicts to the surface will allow them to begin to lead lives that are fulfilling, emotionally satisfying, sexually free and joyful, and existentially comforting.

While not about the existential lives of women, I would anticipate that this book will be of interest to those women who have often found themselves perplexed by the fused relationship between a man and his penis. Women have existential concerns and dilemmas of their own, but this book may shed light on the sexuality of the men they interact with (sexually and nonsexually) in a way that will make interpersonal relationships more satisfying and fulfilling.

This is not a book about political correctness. Neither is it a book that attempts to encourage political incorrectness. This perspective will be especially resonant in Chapter 6, "When Men Behave Badly." This chapter is not about excusing the egregious sexual behavior of men. Rather, it is an attempt to better understand why it is that men do these offending actions. Typically, our approach to men in these situations is to denounce and punish. While punishment is often appropriate, it is rarely helpful in creating "better" men. An understanding of these factors, particularly the existential ones, may help us better understand and treat the underlying issues that lead to inappropriate acting out.

This is a book about men and what drives them. This is a book about men and what confounds them. This is a book about that which what I believe is common to men of all races, religions, and sexual orientations. This is a book about men and how to free them from the constraints of existentially conflicted living. Too ambitious? Perhaps, but I don't think so. I have seen the application of existential psychotherapy principles to the treatment of men's sexual problems result in extraordinary and wonderful changes for many of my patients. Many men whose sexual problems did not respond to other forms of psychotherapy or other therapeutic medical approaches have found that long-elusive happiness by being more aware of the depth of their feelings and learning how to resolve unexplored and poorly integrated childhood trauma.

Of course, no book can be as inclusive as an author would like. While my clinical work has been racially and ethnically diverse, most of my patients were heterosexual, cisgender males. There are men of cultures and sexualities that I know little about. This book reflects my experiences with those men I have worked with, and the clinical vignettes herein are representative of those encounters. We all have blind spots that we've yet to recognize. Even after all my years of doing psychotherapy, I still am learning about the complexities of the human condition. Any omissions are not designed to be negations of the male experience that is representative of cultures or sexualities that are unfamiliar to me. I, like all of us, am a work in progress. My horizons are ever expanding.

There is a slide I often show during many of my lectures. I'm sure many of you have seen it. The slide attempts to highlight the differences between men and women. The top of the slide purports to represent women. Women are portrayed by a series of dials, buttons, switches—38 in all, while men are represented on the bottom portion of the slide by one single toggle switch (in the "up" or "erect" position!). The implication is that female sexuality, as evidenced by the multitude of dials, buttons, and switches, is complicated, whereas male sexuality, as designated as a single toggle switch (in an "erect" position no less), is simple, uncomplicated, and unsophisticated. The slide typically gets chuckles from the audience, but I don't show it for its comedic value. I show it in order to make the point that nothing could be further from the truth than what is implied in this slide. Male sexuality is every bit as complicated, nuanced, and mature as female sexuality, yet it is often seen as being shallow and adolescent. It is time to challenge this perception and recognize that male sexuality is rife with existential meaning and implications. The relationship between a man and his penis is profound and consequential. It is my hope that by the time you reach the end of this book, your understanding and appreciation of men and their sexuality will be expanded and deepened.

The penis speaks. Let us begin to understand what it is saying.

1

THE PENIS SPEAKS

An Existential View of Male Sexual Dysfunction

It is hardly a stretch to suggest that men often obsess over their penis. No other part of the male body receives as much consideration or can provide as much comfort and soothing as a man's genitalia. Men are frequently touching their penis, adjusting their penis, scratching their penis and scrotum, and inspecting their penis. Many have even assigned their penis a pet name. It is not unusual to hear a man refer to his penis with a name like "Mr. Happy," "Action Jackson," "Moby Dick" or "The Big Dipper." Men are also very protective of their penis. Recall from the Introduction that many male combat vets often chide that the first thing they do after an explosion is check to be sure their genitals are intact. Some may remember the reaction among men when in 1993, Lorena Bobbitt severed her husband's penis and tossed it into a field. Even though Lorena had accused her husband of the horrendous crimes of rape and assault, men winced and shivered at the thought of having a penis brutally amputated, regardless of the reason, and could vicariously feel John Wayne Bobbitt's pain, angst, and vulnerability. It is highly

DOI: 10.4324/9781003127871-2

doubtful that the reaction would have been the same had Lorena cut off John Wayne's finger, hand, or even his arm.

While much of the attention paid to the penis may be for the purposes of sexual pleasure, much of it is not. Men who sit on the couch with their hand on their penis are often not looking for sexual arousal or pleasure. They are not having sexual thoughts or fantasies. Indeed, they are probably completely unaware of where their hand may be while they are watching television, reading, etc.

So why such attention? What is the function of the penis (besides the sexual) for so many men? The essential thesis of this book is that the penis is a conduit for male emotion and thus regulates the closeness/distance that men will allow themselves to experience in intimate relationships. While men often pay a great deal of conscious attention to their penis, the unconscious messages our penis sends us can be much more profound and difficult to decipher. In this way, the penis "speaks" for many men who are dealing with repressed, unacknowledged, or unexpressed emotions. Of course, the penis doesn't actually speak (although it is often said in jest that the penis seems to have a mind of its own!). Rather, it is the means through which we are being alerted that we are in a situation that doesn't feel safe, genuine, or secure. In other words, a central tenet of this book is the notion that our unconscious will speak to us through our penis and self-protectively disrupt a sexual interaction due to some perceived danger or threat. Existentially, we are being alerted to a situation that imperils or jeopardizes our literal or emotional *existence*.

The case of James gives us an opportunity to observe how this unfolds.

The Case of James

James was a 53-year-old married heterosexual man who came to see me for erectile dysfunction. He was referred by his urologist, who was quite certain that James's sexual difficulties were psychological in nature. James had recently married for the third time following two unwanted divorces. He reported that he had never experienced erectile difficulties before, and he and his current wife had enjoyed a very nice, spontaneous sex life for the 4 years they dated before marriage. To the surprise of them both, James was unable to maintain penile erection on their honeymoon. That was two years ago, and James's erectile difficulties continued.

By way of history, James reported that he married his first wife while they were both college students. He recalls being "madly" in love with his wife and enjoyed married life greatly. However, after approximately 3 years of marriage, James came home unexpectedly one afternoon and found his wife in bed having sex with one of her co-workers. James was devastated. He was taken completely by surprise, and he was further stunned to hear his wife say that while she was very sorry he had to find out this way, she was unhappy in the marriage and wanted to divorce. She felt they had married too young, and she wanted to experience more of the world before being tied to a relationship. James was crushed and swore to himself that he would never fall in love again and resigned himself to a life of solitary loneliness. He doubted he would ever find happiness again.

However, as time passed, James's pain faded, and his mood improved. To his great delight, he met another woman and, once again, fell madly in love. They dated for about a year and then married. James recalled feeling "deliriously" happy and was again enjoying married life. Unfortunately, after approximately 6 years of marriage, James's second wife also asked for a divorce. James, speechless once again, was overcome with sadness and disbelief. He was angry with his wife for "blindsiding" him but also angry and frustrated with himself for allowing himself to be in this situation again. He renewed his vow to live a life of peaceful aloneness and spare himself the pain and vulnerability of being abandoned in the future.

James continued in this manner for approximately 7 years before he found the woman who would become his third and current wife. James's current wife was a co-worker who helped bring him out of his depressed state, and he unexpectedly found himself falling in love yet again. This time, however, James promised himself he would move slowly and cautiously. After 4 years of dating, the relationship was going quite well, and they decided to marry. James was very pleased to have another chance at love and happiness, and he eagerly anticipated the wedding date. As mentioned above, sex for the couple was effortless, frequent, and satisfying. However, on the first night of their honeymoon, James, for the first time in his adult life, was unable to maintain penile erection. He was perplexed but thought he may have just been exhausted from the excitement of the wedding and travel to their honeymoon destination. However, sex the next day produced the same result. James was able to achieve erection without difficulty, but as the couple went to engage in sexual intercourse, his erection faded. This pattern continued, unabated, for 2 years before James sought medical consultation.

As we began psychotherapy, James related much of what was just described in the preceding paragraphs. One day, as our session was ending, James said, "I don't know if this is important or not, but . . ." I think every experienced psychotherapist knows what that kind of statement portends! James revealed that when he was a very young child, his mother would often "disappear" for prolonged periods of time. Apparently, James's mother suffered from severe depressive episodes. This was in an era before the current wave of antidepressant medications and the interference of health insurance companies pushing for short hospital stays. As a result, James's mother was hospitalized for her depression on several occasions, many lasting for weeks or months. James recalled being a toddler and wandering from room to room in search of his mother. Given his youthful age, his elders didn't think he should be told the truth and exposed to the reality of the situation, so he was told only that his mother had to go away for a while and would soon be back. James recollects this as being a very frightening time, and he often cried in anguish, fearing he would never see his mother again.

James was baffled as to what was causing his erectile shutdown. But this picture was becoming increasingly clear to me. James's penis was speaking to him, but he wasn't understanding the message. Often, the primary task in sex therapy with men is helping the man understand the significance, or meaning, of what his penis is attempting to alert him to. This is what sex therapists often refer to as "penis wisdom." The concept of penis wisdom suggests that there are times when the penis (representing the messages generated in the unconscious) perceives a danger that the conscious mind is unaware of. When this occurs, the force of the unconscious will overpower the wishes of the conscious. The result is a sexual shutdown that is designed to protect the man from a potentially threatening situation.

Let's examine another case in which the penis speaks.

The Case of Edward

Edward was a 55-year-old widowed man who consulted with me for concerns about erectile dysfunction. Edward reported that his wife of 32 years died two years ago after an extended and excruciatingly painful bout with cancer. He was her primary caretaker during her illness and spent his days tending to her every wish and need. He missed her terribly. About a year ago, he met a new woman and, to his amazement, found love again. He was surprised to find how comfortable he was with her and how much he enjoyed their time together. This included an uncomplicated and highly enjoyable sexual life. The couple was planning to marry in the next year, but as the wedding date approached, Edward began to experience erectile difficulties for the first time in his adult life. As with James, Edward reported achieving penile erection spontaneously and effortlessly. He would be able to maintain his erection for extended periods of foreplay but would then detumesce as they approached sexual intercourse or shortly after penile insertion. Edward was completely befuddled by this situation, and this pattern continued up to the time we first met.

In therapy, Edward revealed that he and his soon-to-be wife had decided to sell their individual homes and purchase a home together. Both seemed to think this was a wise course of action, as it would give them a fresh start in a new marital relationship. Neither wanted to be burdened with living in the other's home beside the "ghost" of a previous spouse. Edward, however, was puzzled as to why he had continued to procrastinate on preparing his house for sale. Indeed, since the death of his wife over 2 years ago, he had not moved or changed a thing in his house. He hadn't moved any furniture, changed any pictures, or begun to pack up his deceased wife's clothing, jewelry, or toiletries. In addition, Edward had confined himself to only three rooms in the rather large house they had shared: the bedroom, kitchen, and den. I queried him about what this might mean, but he was rather dismissive that his delay held much meaning beyond the fact that he was a busy person and just hadn't found the time. He vowed to make significant progress before our next meeting.

When Edward returned the next week, he rather sheepishly admitted that he had made no progress whatsoever in the dismantling of his

home. His avoidance of the task continued for the next 3 weeks, until
Edward had little choice but to accept and confront the source of his
ambivalence. He finally acknowledged that while he very much loved
his wife-to-be and wanted to marry her, he couldn't help but feel he was
"cheating" on his former spouse. He recognized the irrationality of this
and even recalled his deceased wife telling him as she was dying that he
was still a young man, and it would be her wish that he remarry in the
future. Nevertheless, Edward could not shake the guilt and anxiety he
experienced whenever he contemplated packing up the house. He also
came to realize that he was not yet finished mourning his first wife, and
the idea of disrupting the space she once physically occupied with him
aroused intense emotions that he found difficult to verbalize or express.

Edward's situation is hardly uncommon in widowed men. Indeed,
authors such as Schover (1984) and Watter (1994, 1998) have written about the phenomenon known as the Widower's Syndrome. The
Widower's Syndrome refers to a pattern in which a man experiences substantial difficulty in resuming sex after the death of his spouse/partner.
In the classic picture, the spouse/partner suffers from a lingering, painful illness, and the couple is often unable to have sex for many months or
even years. Following the spouse/partner's death, the man will attempt
sexual intercourse with a new partner only to find that for the first time
in his life, he is unable to maintain penile erection. Levine (1988) has
suggested that it is reasonable for the sex therapist to presume that erectile problems in widowed men may involve internal conflicts related to
unresolved grief, guilt about having a new partner, and/or a sense that
he belongs only to his deceased spouse/partner. Interestingly, in the case
of Edward, he did not experience any erectile problems when beginning
to have sex with his new partner. Rather, his erectile difficulties began
as he was nearing the wedding date and beginning to disassemble the
home he shared with his first wife.

Once again, we are witness to how the penis speaks. Edward had no
conscious idea as to why his penis was shutting down, as the source of
the problem likely lies deep within his unconscious mind. However,
such explorations have not typically been the primary interventions in
sex therapy. Rather, the focus for engagement in sex therapy would identify the fears of performance James and Edward were experiencing. Sex
therapy has traditionally assumed that performance anxiety is at the root

of male sexual dysfunction. As a result, sex therapy would customarily presuppose that both James and Edward were experiencing erectile loss because they were so consumed with performance fears or performance anxiety that they would be unable to maintain their arousal to continue in sexual activity. As a result, the overwhelming majority of sex therapists would most likely proceed with interventions designed to reduce performance anxiety with the belief that by doing so, they would restore satisfactory penile functioning.

Let's examine the concept of performance anxiety more closely.

The Emphasis on "Performance Anxiety"

As mentioned previously, sex therapists have traditionally understood sexual dysfunction, especially male sexual dysfunction, as stemming from a phenomenon referred to as "performance anxiety." Performance anxiety was introduced into sex therapy by William H. Masters and Virginia E. Johnson in their groundbreaking text, Human Sexual Inadequacy (Masters & Johnson, 1970). According to Masters and Johnson, the fear of not being able to perform sexually is the paramount sexual concern of men. As a consequence of trying to "will" an involuntary physiological response (i.e., erection), the man essentially blocks himself from the naturally occurring reaction to effective sexual stimuli. Once his penis does not respond in a sexual situation as he would expect, he becomes an acute observer of penile reactivity. The man then assumes the role of "spectator" and becomes over-focused on the function (or lack thereof) of his penis. The result is an ongoing cycle of negative expectation, anxiety about performance, spectatoring, and erectile failure.

These ideas were further developed by psychiatrist Helen Singer Kaplan. In her influential text The New Sex Therapy, (Kaplan, 1974), Kaplan asserts that the anticipation of being unable to perform sexually may be the greatest immediate cause of male erectile dysfunction and orgasmic dysfunction as well. While she does acknowledge that performance anxiety is not the only potential causative factor in male sexual problems, she confirms the belief that it is, by far, the most common. She further suggests that it is certainly a major factor in the maintenance of the cycle of erectile failure, regardless of the initial cause. With regard to treatment, Kaplan believes that reducing the fear of sexual performance, as well as the concomitant spectatoring, are essential primary goals of the effective treatment of male sexual dysfunction.

The emphasis on performance anxiety as having a central role in the creation and maintenance of male sexual dysfunction has continued to the present day. Most every sex therapy text that examines the phenomenon of male sexual problems will identify the alleviation of performance anxiety as a major goal of effective sex therapy. While logical sounding and widely accepted without question, the role of performance anxiety has largely gone unexamined over the years. Take, for example, a recent article by Pyke (2020) in which he purports to examine the diagnostic utility of performance anxiety in male sexual dysfunction. Noting that there are few studies assessing the efficacy of treatment for what he refers to as sexual performance anxiety, or SPA, Pyke ultimately concludes that there are no well-proven treatments yet proclaims that SPA causes or maintains most common sexual dysfunctions. Here again, the validity and utility of performance anxiety as the major cause of male sexual dysfunction are given further legitimacy and authority without it ever really being questioned or examined.

I believe that while it can be persuasively and effectively argued that performance anxiety may play a significant role in the *maintenance* of male sexual dysfunction, its role as a causative or etiological factor in such problems is incomplete and underdeveloped. Most of the cases of male sexual dysfunction that I have seen do not appear to be caused by a fear of or anxiety about performance. A typical presentation in my practice is a man who has a long history of unimpeded and nonproblematic sexual functioning (often including with his current partner) and spontaneously develops a cycle of erectile failure following a *relationship-deepening event*. Relationship-deepening events can be any significant indicator that the relationship is becoming more serious and the risk of emotional vulnerability has intensified. These are the cases that often present with the statements, "Sex was great until we moved in together." Or "Sex was great until we married." Or "Sex was great until we had our first child." The list goes on and on, depending upon what circumstance threatens the existence of the man and triggers the sexual shutdown. Even though these sexual complications appear to occur spontaneously, in reality, they have been simmering beneath the man's conscious awareness for quite some time. Of note is that this pattern often includes little to no difficulty achieving penile erection and maintaining that erection during what are often extended periods of foreplay. Masturbation is no problem, and fellatio is also often unimpeded. However, just prior to or quickly following intromission, his erection fades. Certainly, fears of performance failure are impactful going forward, but just how impactful are they? Given such a presentation, it is my belief that male sexual dysfunction is most often caused by anxiety, but that anxiety is not rooted in performance fears. There is clearly something that is specific to intercourse and the meaning given to intercourse that has rattled both James and Edward. And it is the meaning that sexual intercourse has at this point in their lives, since intromission was never a problem before. One of the central precepts of this book is that most of male sexual dysfunction is the result of the triggering of an earlier trauma. The following section will examine the role of trauma, particularly early childhood trauma, in the creation of an existential crisis and the etiology of male sexual dysfunction.

The Role of Trauma and Male Sexual Dysfunction

According to the American Psychiatric Association (2000), trauma is defined as an event that is experienced or witnessed, presents a threat to one's physical or psychological safety, and to which a person responds with intense feelings of fear, helplessness, or shock. I would add that such events pose a threat to one's core *existence* and the meaning they ascribe to their essential purpose in life.

Studies have demonstrated that exposure to early childhood adversity, such as trauma, can have a profound negative impact on adult mental health (Merrick et al., 2017). In addition, Hillis et al. (2001) and Brown et al. (2015) have found that adverse childhood experiences have a strong effect on the development of problematic sexual behavior. However, most of our research on the effects of trauma on sexual behavior has focused on the impact of *sexual* trauma and its potential for disrupting adult sexuality. While it is clear that traumas such as sexual abuse and sexual assault can result in severe sexual problems going forward, the role that nonsexual traumas may have on sexual behavior has gone largely unexamined. It has been my experience that the triggering of nonsexual trauma is often at the root of adult sexual problems. More on this in a bit.

Among the few who have considered nonsexual traumas and their impact on adult sexual behavior are Levenson et al. (2017). Most of Levenson and her colleagues' work has been with sex offenders, not sexual dysfunction, yet much of what they say is applicable to both groups. They have suggested viewing problematic sexual behavior through the lens of a trauma-informed eye. They believe that when viewed through the lens of trauma, such behaviors are better conceptualized as symptoms rather than problems. They suggest that much of childhood trauma results in a state of perpetual hyperarousal, and when children grow up constantly scanning the environment for danger, they are primed to expect threats to their safety and to respond accordingly.

They have also observed:

> Some childhood traumas are rather overt, like physical and sexual abuse or witnessing domestic violence. Other experiences like emotional neglect, an absent parent, or a substance abusing caretaker may be harder to identify but are often chronic and lead to subtle and insidious impacts. For instance, some people have parents who were well intentioned but smothering, and they grow up needing to push people away because being close to others means that you can't have your own identity. Early losses can generate pseudomaturity or parentification in children, which can promote positive qualities like leadership and confidence, but can also mean difficulties asking for or accepting help.
>
> (p. 14)

Trauma-informed practitioners understand that signs and symptoms of trauma often masquerade as presenting problems in therapy. In addition, Levenson et al. suggest that oftentimes when considering trauma victims, their problematic behavior represents a protection against vulnerability. Their observations very closely mirror my clinical experience.

In many of the cases of male sexual dysfunction that I've treated, I have conceptualized the sexual shutdown as a protective reaction to the triggering of an earlier trauma. If one subscribes to the theory of a protective unconscious, many sexual dysfunctions can be understood as the protective unconscious sounding an alarm that is designed to alert the man that he may be engaging in an activity that might place him in a dangerous and extremely vulnerable position. This alarm, then, communicates through the penis that the man may be placing himself in a precarious situation and, although his conscious mind is telling him to move forward, his unconscious mind seeks to protect him from excess vulnerability by pulling him back at the moment of greatest connection and fusion with another body. In this way, the penis speaks. The penis reflects our protective unconscious's hyperarousal or constant scanning of the environment for potential dangers. Other authors have also spoken to the idea that our genitals or other body parts speak for us to protect us from unconsciously perceived dangers (Kleinplatz, 2003a). As Yalom (2008) has observed, "The pain is there; when you close one door on it, it knocks to come in somewhere else" (p. 55).

Of course, the man is unaware of what is occurring in his unconscious mind, and often fails to associate his body's reaction with past trauma. If we recall Levenson et al.'s comment that when considered from the perspective of trauma, behaviors are considered as symptoms rather than problems, we get a clearer picture of why and how the penis speaks. This would suggest that most sexual problems are not really about sex per se but rather are a symptom of some underlying condition that is being expressed in a sexual manner. When the trauma is relational, what better means of expression of fears of vulnerability than a protective sexual distancing or shutdown?

In her wonderful book *The Drama of the Gifted Child: The Search for the True Self*, Alice Miller (1981) has discerned that early childhood trauma can set the stage for our adult reactions when that trauma is triggered. Miller says:

> The damage done to us during childhood cannot be undone, since we cannot change anything in our past. We can, however, change ourselves. We can repair ourselves and gain our lost integrity by choosing to look more closely at the knowledge that is stored inside our bodies and bringing this knowledge closer to our awareness. This path, although certainly not easy, is the only route by which we can at last leave behind the cruel, invisible prison of our childhood. We become free by transforming ourselves from unaware victims of the past into responsible individuals in the present, who are aware of our past and are thus able to live with it.
>
> Of course, most people do exactly the opposite. Without realizing that the past is constantly determining their present actions, they avoid learning anything about their history. They continue to live

in their repressed childhood situation, ignoring the fact that it no longer exists. They are continuing to fear and avoid dangers that, although once real, have not been real for a long time. They are driven by unconscious memories and by repressed feelings and needs that determine nearly everything they do or fail to do.

(pp. 1–2)

Miller points out that we are often unaware of how our childhood reactions to traumatic circumstances can manifest themselves when that trauma is triggered in adulthood. The trauma lies deep within us and we, unaware, continue to live the present as if it were the same as the past. As a result, unless the trauma imbedded in our unconscious mind is brought to our conscious awareness, we will continue to repeat the same dysfunctional patterns over and over.

Similarly, Levenson and her colleagues suggest,

> by shifting the paradigm to view client problems as symptoms of well-rehearsed responses to traumagenic experiences, we can begin to conceptualize treatment not as 'what's wrong with you?' but 'what happened to you?' In this way, we can understand the meaning attached to those experiences which profoundly shaped the ways clients think about themselves and others, and how they contribute to their expectations that the world is not a safe place. We can reframe client behaviors as a set of skills that were once adaptive in a threatening early environment but now tend to interfere with the client reaching his personal goals and establishing intimate connections with others.

(p. 17)

Levenson et al. remind us that much of what occurs when early trauma is triggered is engaging in protective patterns that may have been the best and most effective strategies available to us as children, but are no longer helpful or efficacious when we are adults and have more available options.

Trauma psychiatrist Bessel Van Der Kolk takes this a step further and observes that much of the psychological sequalae of our trauma is stored in our physical bodies. He suggests:

> the bodies of incest victims have trouble distinguishing between danger and safety. This means that the imprint of past trauma does not consist only of distorted perceptions of

information coming from the outside; the organism itself also has a problem knowing how to feel safe. The past is impressed not only on their minds, and in misinterpretations of innocuous events, but also on the very core of their beings: in the safety of their bodies.

(p. 129)

Van Der Kolk reminds us that our bodies can often speak in an attempt to protect us from perceived danger. However, since the memories that our bodies store for us are outside of our conscious awareness, we often are oblivious to the fact that our body is trying to send us a message and to the meaning behind the message our body is attempting to convey.

With the comments of Levenson, Miller, and Van Der Kolk in mind, let's return to the cases of James and Edward. If we look closely at the cases of James and Edward, it would seem to be quite apparent that the likelihood of their difficulties being the result of performance fears or performance anxiety would be, at best, incomplete. Both James and Edward reported long histories of nonproblematic erectile functioning, not only in prior relationships but within the relationships in which they were now experiencing difficulty. James and Edward both had several years of spontaneous, relaxed, frequent, and enjoyable sexual interactions with their current partners. So why would they suddenly develop performance fears? Why now? Given their long histories of sexual success, why would they be unable to brush off an erectile loss as an aberration? Or as nothing to be overly concerned about?

The answer must lie within the depths of their unconscious minds, deep beyond the observable concerns about performance. It is my belief that for both James and Edward, their current circumstances triggered the fears from earlier traumas that threatened their sense of safety. Indeed, such fears give rise to existential concerns that endanger their very existence.

Let's consider one additional case in which the penis communicates an alert that screams of existential conflict and distress.

The Case of David

David was a 38-year-old, single, gay man who came to see me due to his concern about delayed ejaculation. David reported that he had been struggling with this condition for many years. He had tried therapy in the past, but without any alleviation of his symptoms.

Most sex therapists will acknowledge that delayed ejaculation has historically been one of the most perplexing male sexual problems and one of the most difficult to treat. Over the years, this condition has gone by various names, including ejaculatory impotence (Kaplan & Abrams, 1958), retarded ejaculation (Masters & Johnson, 1970), ejaculatory incompetence (Newell, 1978), ejaculatory inhibition (McCarthy & Metz, 2007), male orgasmic disorder (APA, 2000), and the current delayed ejaculation (Perelman & Watter, 2014, 2016). The frequent name changes speak to the diagnostic confusion and the complexities of this disorder. Delayed ejaculation is often unresponsive to the traditional behaviorally based sex therapy techniques. As a result, it is hardly a surprise that David had found little relief from his earlier therapies.

David explained that his ejaculatory difficulties had plagued him for many years. However, he reported that his difficulties only occurred in relationships that seemed to have the potential to get serious. He had no trouble ejaculating during one-night stands with anonymous partners, and solo masturbation was also effortless. When he met a new man, sex would start out fine, but if the relationship continued beyond a couple of dates, ejaculation would no longer be possible. Naturally, David was flummoxed as to the reason for his ejaculatory changes, and his prior therapies spent little time in exploring the possible meaning behind his presenting complaint.

David recalled a highly traumatized upbringing. His mother, who was an active drug addict, worked as a prostitute to obtain money for drugs. David was conceived by a customer of his mother's, and the identity of his father was unknown. David had four half siblings, all born under similar circumstances with different fathers. David's mother's drug addiction meant that she was often absent for days or weeks, and David and his siblings were often left alone. Eventually, child protective services became involved, and the children were each placed in different foster homes. Eventually, an aunt and uncle adopted three of the kids but not David. David was never clear as to why his aunt and uncle didn't take him as well, and he was filled with rage and often acted out. After approximately 5 years, his aunt and uncle brought him into their family, but his rage, resentment, and feelings of rejection and low self-worth never left him. He was not an easy child and wanted to be reunited with his mother. David's mother would occasionally show up, profess her love for him, and promise to get a house where they could live together. Needless to say, she consistently disappointed David, always leaving him waiting by the door with bags packed and ready, waiting for the mother that never came to get him.

As an adult, David was highly accomplished. He was a successful dermatologist with a thriving practice. However, his social life was unsatisfying and problematic. He had few friends, and all his long-term relationships fell apart. David was deeply untrusting and was always testing those he was involved with. He fully expected that others would disappoint or abandon him, and he had vowed to be certain to sabotage any promising relationship before the other person could break up with him.

It was clear to me that David's sexual and relational difficulties were the result of his traumatic childhood. As a child, he had learned to expect caretakers to be unreliable and rejecting. He unconsciously became an environmental scanner and expected to see signs of betrayal, duplicity, and disillusionment around every corner. When considered from the perspective of a self-protective unconscious, what better signal from the penis could there be than the unwillingness to fully let go (i.e., ejaculate) if you see such danger in the environment around you? As mentioned in the introduction, the penis is the primary conduit for male emotion and, as such, becomes the regulator of the amount of closeness/distance a man will be able to tolerate and allow. For David, his traumatic childhood has prepared him to expect that others will injure him, and his protective unconscious attempts to shield him from the expected vicissitudes of life.

The Symbolism of the Penis

Thus far, we have explored the means by which the penis speaks and the notion that much of male sexual dysfunction is the result of unexplored, unacknowledged, and unexpressed trauma. Now, we need to go a bit deeper into our exploration of male sexual problems. What types of traumas result in sexual shutdowns? Why don't all men who have had traumatic childhoods experience sexual difficulties?

It is my assertion that the etiology for much of male sexual conflict lies within the realm of traumas that impact not only the lives of men but, more specifically, the existential lives of men. We're looking at traumas that attack and threaten the very core of our existence. These traumas are insidious and lie beneath our level of awareness, and one of the fundamental tasks for existential psychotherapy is to increase our awareness of our existence and threats to that existence. The late existential psychologist Rollo May (1953) has suggested, "Certain values . . . are believed in as the 'core' of the person's reason for living, and if such a value is destroyed, the person feels his existence as a self might as well be destroyed likewise" (p. 24). Existential psychotherapy is concerned with helping people discover what it means to them to be alive, to live meaningful lives, and have strong, connected relationships. For many men, the penis is their path to living a life of such substance. A fully functional penis is central to their sense of wholeness, desirability, belonging, and connection. Why the penis as opposed to some other body part? Psychiatrist Irvin Yalom (2002a) suggests that sex is the vital life force, and as such, it often counters existential fears, particularly the terror of death. A fully functioning penis represents being vital and alive, whereas a compromised penis represents a loss of vitality, strength, and being.

It is important to note that from an existential perspective, some traumas are much less obvious than others. Traumas such as parental loss, neglect, or substance abuse are fairly easy to identify and understand. What is more complicated and often more deeply hidden are the messages that get buried in the unconscious mind. Not all men who have existential trauma have experienced the obvious losses that were illustrated in the cases of James, Edward, and David. Some have lived lives in which more subtle relational effects have instilled in them the terror and dread of the consequences of expressing emotion, particularly negative emotion. Here, I'm referring to those men who have suffered the hidden traumas of fearful, anxious, overprotective, or emotionally volatile parents or caretakers that they have learned to "dance around" so as not to upset them and disrupt the home environment. These are men who stuff emotions down deep inside and are often unaware that they are even experiencing them. However, while they may not be aware of or able to acknowledge the existence of such emotional turmoil, those emotions will, when the circumstances are such that they are triggered, find their way out and demand expression. In areas of relational emotional conflict, the penis speaks. It is often the man's penis that delivers the message of distress. The penis must speak because the conscious and direct expression of these negative emotions threatens the safety or core existence of these men. However, we are getting a bit ahead of ourselves. We will return to this notion and discuss it in greater detail in Chapter 4. But first, let's look at the fundamental principles of existential therapy and the work of Irvin D. Yalom, M.D.

2

EXISTENTIAL PSYCHOTHERAPY AND THE WORK OF IRVIN D. YALOM, M.D.

Existential psychotherapy is comprised of a richly diverse grouping of theories and practices. Deeply rooted in the teachings of philosophy, existential psychotherapy aims to illuminate the way in which people come to choose, create, and perpetuate their own way of being in the world. Primary importance is placed on the here-and-now in relationships, both in and out of the consultation room, and the therapy seeks to assist individuals in navigating the existential vagaries of their existence. The overall purpose of existential therapy, then, is to help patients find meaning in life and their existential situation (Lantz, 1993) and allow clients to explore their lives honestly, openly, and comprehensively (Cooper et al., 2019).

Overview of the Foundations of Existential Psychotherapy

While all existential psychotherapists share some aspects of a similar vision of existential therapy, there is a great deal of diversity in terms of

DOI: 10.4324/9781003127871-3

approach, design, and practice.[1] For example, there are those practitioners who see existential psychotherapy as a distinct and specific school
of therapy, while others see the principles of existential psychotherapy
as a "lens" that can be incorporated into many different forms of psychotherapy. What is common among existential therapists include the
mentioned here-and-now focus, or what Spinelli (1997) refers to as
the "lived immediacy" of the therapeutic encounter, as well as a deep
commitment to the importance of a genuine, honest, collaborative, and
connected therapeutic relationship. Existential psychotherapy is a profoundly human, person-centered approach to the psychotherapy process, and existential therapists believe that therapy is guided primarily
by the relationship between therapist and patient, as opposed to being
directed by theory, technique, imprecise and arbitrary diagnostic labels,
or anything else that limits our ability to see the uniqueness and individuality of the person behind the presenting symptom. It should be no
surprise, then, that existential psychotherapy defies a simple definition,
as the essence of existential psychotherapy eschews all that is limiting.

Existential psychotherapy has its roots in philosophy, and much of
its foundation is built upon the works of Nietzsche, Heidegger, Sartre,
Socrates, Freud, Schopenhauer, Kierkegaard, Kant, Buber, and Camus to
name but a few. As such, existential psychotherapy attempts to understand the human condition more from the vantage point of a philosophical appreciation of humanity, as opposed to the more "medicalized" view
of the human experience that is common in much of psychotherapy
today. Indeed, I have often told my graduate students and psychotherapy
trainees that in order to appreciate the breadth and depth of the human
condition, they would do well to not spend all of their time reading
solely psychology texts and journals. Novelists and philosophers often
have a much fuller and richer understanding of human suffering and frequently have more to teach us than do those who base their understanding of people on structured and, by definition, limited research design
and data. Nobel Prize recipient Elie Wiesel has been quoted as saying,
"It is not enough to know the facts. We must take things—history, current events—personally. We must look in mirrors. And great literature
can act as a mirror" (Burger, 2018). Wiesel believed that great books
could serve as tools of increased self-awareness. They become vehicles
through which we learn about ourselves and our psychological and

ethical natures. As such, the existentially minded psychotherapist will spend a great deal of time immersing themselves in the literary works of Dickens, Tolstoy, Hemingway, Roth, Dostoyevsky, Kafka, Ibsen, Woolf, Proust, Joyce, and Cervantes, as well as the cogitations of psychotherapists such as Yalom, May, Frankl, Szasz, Laing, Fromm, and so many others who have thoughtfully reflected on the practical and existential struggles common to humans. Reading the works of these authors will help create a greater awareness of the depth and emotionality of human turmoil than will most any scientific publication. Of course, the notion that psychotherapy can be robustly influenced by great philosophical and literary works is hardly new. According to Lehrman (1940), on the occasion of being honored on his 70th birthday as the discoverer of the unconscious, Freud disclaimed the title and famously said, "The poets and philosophers before me discovered the unconscious. What I discovered was the scientific method by which the unconscious can be studied." This is not to suggest that psychology texts and journals are not of great benefit to psychotherapists. I and most of my colleagues have gleaned much of our knowledge of human behavior from the scientific endeavor. However, given the restrictions of design required for scientific rigor, much of the nuance and substance of the human condition is lost in experimentally based research texts and presentations.

Existential psychotherapy is a therapy best suited for the "curious." It is essential that both patient and therapist be keenly interested in the personal development and evolution of the individual, his/her/their story, and be willing to explore the unexamined darkness of life (i.e., the concept of mortality as an example). Personally, I have been curious for as long as I can remember. Of course, this has not always been a good thing. I recall an incident in first grade in which my teacher, who was an otherwise wonderful woman, selected me to bring an envelope down to the principal's office. I was honored and so proud to have been selected, and when I walked to the front of the room to receive the missive, I asked, "What is it?" My teacher then abruptly turned and asked someone else in the class to take the envelope to the principal. It is obvious to me that this incident was one of great impact given I still can recall the confusion, embarrassment, and surprise I felt. Her message was received— questioning was not welcomed. However, rather than quell my curiosity, this event only served to provoke it, although I suspect I restrained much of my curiosity until I got to second grade!

For me, existential psychotherapy was a perfect fit. I love stories, people's stories, and have found myself captivated by observing and sharing in the unfolding of a person's life narrative through a course of deep psychotherapy. People often ask how I (and my colleagues) can sit with people, all day long, day after day, and listen to so much human struggle and unhappiness? I have never found this to be a burden. I become deeply entranced when hearing about people's lives and engrossed in examining how they navigate the struggle to find meaningful relationships. The psychotherapist's interest and attention to a patient's life can be, in and of itself, enormously therapeutic. So many of those who seek us out feel lonely, unworthy, and invisible. For the existential psychotherapist, the efficacy and utility of the here-and-now focus and the use and the power of the therapeutic relationship is unparalleled in fostering the healing of the patient's wounds and existential aloneness.

People most often come in for psychotherapy due to their relationship concerns and difficulties. Existential psychotherapy is intensely relationship focused, and the belief of many existential philosophers and therapists is that relationships are central to human existence. Spinelli (1997) suggests that existential theory insists on viewing human beings from a *relational* rather than an isolated perspective. Van Deurzen & Iacovou (2013b) have persuasively posited that individuality is secondary to relationship, as we are never fully separate from the world around us. The existential psychotherapist believes that the same problems that occur in people's relationships outside the consultation room will become readily apparent during the course of psychotherapy. Of course, this is true of many forms of psychotherapy, but what separates the existential school of psychotherapy from other schools of thought is the way in which the psychotherapy relationship is utilized as the primary tool for healing. The therapeutic relationship is the most potent, formidable, and effective tool in the existential therapist's armamentarium. It is principally for this reason that the existential psychotherapist is acutely aware of the therapy "process." That is, by focusing on the here-and-now relationship between the patient and therapist, the existentially oriented psychotherapist may do his/her/their most powerful work. Given the primacy placed on the therapeutic encounter, the existential therapist is frequently checking in with the patient about how they are experiencing the psychotherapy process and what is happening in the space between therapist and patient. "How are you feeling about what has occurred between us today?" is one of the most important questions an existential therapist will ask. Similarly, in existential couples' therapy, questions such as, "what was it like to listen to your partner's story and to allow yourself to feel what they feel?" and "what have you learned about each other today and how might you take this forward?" are critical to the therapeutic process (van Deurzen, 2013).

It is important to recognize that the patient and therapist will often have very different experiences of the therapeutic encounter. We have all had the experience of a patient coming into a session and telling us that what we said to them during the last session made such a powerful impact, yet we are at a complete loss to know what it is they are referring to. As a result, the existential psychotherapist must also be aware of his/her/their reactions to the therapy encounter. It is for this reason that Yalom (2002a) and others have strongly suggested that psychotherapists be involved in a therapy of their own. The existential psychotherapy relationship is one that is based on an honest, authentic exchange between patient and therapist. It would hardly seem reasonable to ask the patient to be honest and aware if we, ourselves, remain unaware and therefore cannot be authentic and genuine in how we present for our patients.

To foster authenticity in the therapeutic encounter, Yalom (2002a) is a strong proponent of the prudent use of therapist self-disclosure. He sees the patient and therapist as "fellow travelers" and strives to make the therapeutic encounter a mutually engaged process. Of course, the psychotherapist must never lose sight of the fact that the therapeutic encounter must be exclusively for the benefit of the patient and the addressing of the patient's needs, but Yalom is a firm believer that thoughtful therapist disclosure makes the relationship more genuine, authentic, and therapeutic. Indeed, Yalom (2002a) has opined that disclosure begets disclosure. The more the therapist is willing to take risks and be present in a sincere, transparent manner, the greater the likelihood that the patient will feel safe enough to risk being open and forthcoming as well. Naturally, all therapist disclosure should be made judiciously and only for the benefit of the patient, but it is remarkable how much more effective the therapy becomes when the patient views the therapist as someone who is engaged, transparent, authentic, and trustworthy, as opposed to distant, disconnected, and enigmatic.

As mentioned, existential psychotherapy abjures that which limits our examination and understanding of one's life. Existential psychotherapists are extremely critical of the diagnostic process as it currently exists and have often described it as reductionistic and objectifying. According to Barker (2011), diagnosis and treatment on the basis of symptoms miss the *meaning* of these symptoms and behaviors and thus dehumanize the individual. Yalom (2002a) asserts that diagnosis can actually be counter-productive to the psychotherapy process by limiting the therapist's vision and ability to relate to the other as a person in search of understanding. He views the existing diagnostic process as an incomplete attempt to standardize our understanding of human travail and serves only to render the treatment less real and less effective. Both Yalom (2002a) and Szasz (1980) stress that the prevailing notion of psychiatric diagnosis misses the essence of the human being and his/her/their struggle. After all, what experienced psychotherapist would disagree with the observation that it is far easier to assign a DSM V (American Psychiatric Association, 2013) diagnosis after session one than it is after session ten? The more we come to know the other, the more complex and unique their suffering is. Therefore, Yalom (2002a) advocates for the therapist to strive to create a new therapy for each patient. Of course, diagnosis may be necessary to satisfy the reimbursement requirements of a health insurance carrier, but in terms of its impact on the therapy itself, the existential psychotherapist would place minimal importance on the current medically oriented diagnostic process.

The Existential Therapy Experience

In a revealing 2019 article published in the *Atlantic* magazine, Faith Hill (the editor from the *Atlantic*, not the country singer!) discusses her experience of visiting an existential psychotherapist. Hill recalls,

> Occasionally, Jane would stop and ask what I was feeling in the moment. It was a way of sticking to the idea of "presence" that is so essential to existentialists: that you have a responsibility to show up to your life. You can't avoid it, in all its pain and beauty, by living in the past—personal histories and buried traumas matter, and they might inform the present, but it won't do to dwell on them.
>
> And that was it. For an hour, I talked about what it was like for me to be human, and why it often feels so hard. There were no answers—Jane didn't give me any tips for processing mortality, or

ways to make my life feel more meaningful. She didn't tell me I had a purpose, or that I should strengthen connections with friends, or to tell my parents I loved them. After the session ended, I talked with Jane for a bit about her approach. "Part of the existential is just acknowledging "That ship has sailed," she said. "A lot of it is mourning. You mourn these realities so that you can move toward relinquishing them."

She concludes her article with:

When our time was up, Jane ended it directly and firmly. This was part of the approach, she told me—you have to be honest about things. "I don't want to deny that things end brutally," she said. "I can't collude with the idea that there's all the time in the world."

I left the office then, out of the double doors and into the misty afternoon. It was cold for September, but I wanted to walk the hour home. I still had all the same existential concerns—the fear of time, the loneliness, all the myriad uncertainties. But I felt a little lighter, having had these anxieties listened to, and validated. It was a bit like coming across a line in a poem or a quote in a book that you relate to on an eerily intimate level—something of your most personal experience mirrored back to you, and you realize all at once that someone else had had the very same thought. Suddenly and certainly, if only for that moment, you are a little less alone.

Hill's description of an existential psychotherapy session is not atypical. True, different therapists will have differing styles, but in Hill's consultation, you see the close attention to what is happening in the relationship between therapist and patient, the attempts to understand the uniqueness and individuality of Hill's circumstances, and the importance of accepting the current realities of life and effectively mourning the losses of what has passed or not come to pass. While certainly not ahistorical, the existential psychotherapist chooses to use one's personal history as a learning tool or aid in gaining a greater understanding and awareness of why one chooses to live as they do and relate to others as they have. The work, then, is focused on using that newfound insight and awareness to improve their relationship with themselves and those in the world around them. In a sense, one could say the essence of existential psychotherapy is helping the patient to acknowledge and accept the disappointments of the past and to live life going forward with as few regrets as possible.

Another central tenant of existential theory and psychotherapy that is evident in Hill's story is the notion that existential theory places anxiety at its center (Spinelli, 1997; van Deurzen & Iacovou, 2013). Our relationship with ourselves, with others, and with the world around us is inherently anxiety provoking and risky. Anxiety that is avoided or left unacknowledged and unexplored can manifest itself in a variety of problematic feelings and behaviors (including problems of sexuality). An existential therapist will emphasize the importance of tolerating and examining anxiety and seeing it as an inevitable part of our existence as well as a signal (recall the notion of the protective unconscious from Chapter 1) that something in our life requires our focus and attention.

Even though much of existential psychotherapy deals with the darker and more anxiety-provoking topics of life, such as loss, meaninglessness, isolation, and death, existential psychotherapy is, in reality, a decidedly life-affirming process. One of my favorite Yalom quotes is, "Though the physicality of death destroys us, the idea of death may save us" (Yalom, 2002a, 2002b, 2008). While at first glance, this may sound like a rather deflating phrase, it is actually an extraordinarily optimistic reflection of the idea that having an awareness of the unavoidable truths of existence may inspire us to live the life we have going forward in as meaningful a manner as possible. Perhaps this concept is best expressed through a literary reference.

The Existential Angst of Dickens's Ebenezer Scrooge

As mentioned earlier, some of the most poignant illustrations of existential suffering and awareness come to us through the reading of great literature. One of my favorites is the Dickens classic *A Christmas Carol* (Dickens, 1843). In this tale, Dickens relates the story of Ebenezer Scrooge, a miserly curmudgeon who has earned the designation of the most vilified and disliked man in his town. He lives a life of solitary bitterness and exudes a cruel disdain for others who reside in his environs. He is unsympathetic toward those who suffer, often blaming them for their own misfortunes. He hoards his wealth and refuses to be compassionate or charitable to those in need. He is considered a blight on his community, and most have wisely learned to keep their distance from him.

Many of us are acquainted with one or more of the several fine movie versions of this story, but Dickens's written words give us a much more powerful and in-depth understanding of Scrooge, the man. Most of the film versions give us little insight into how Scrooge developed into the man he is, but through the eyes of Dickens, we begin to see Ebenezer Scrooge as a man who has suffered a tremendous amount of early childhood trauma. This unacknowledged and unexplored trauma imprisons him in a lifetime of existential angst and torment. For example, Scrooge is a very wealthy man. Yet not only is he miserly and uncharitable with others, but he affords himself none of the luxuries money can provide. His home, while large, is dreary and bare. He refuses to burn enough coal to adequately heat his home and office, preferring instead to wrap himself in old blankets. He spends little on any of the things that would provide a life of greater comfort for himself and instead chooses a life of deprivation and misery.

Dickens tells us Scrooge's very beginnings were tragic. His mother died while giving birth to him, and his father irrationally blamed poor Ebenezer for taking his adored wife away from him. Scrooge's father was both verbally and physically abusive to young Ebenezer, eventually banishing him from the home and sending him off to a boarding school, where his father essentially abandoned him. Scrooge's father never visited his son nor allowed him to return home for holidays or school recesses. The only person who seemed to care for or about Scrooge was his sister, Fan. Fan would visit him at school, bring him sweet presents, and was unconditionally loving and nurturing toward him. Scrooge deeply loved his sister and saw her as the one source of positivity and happiness in his otherwise isolated, lonely, and woeful existence.

Unfortunately, Fan was tragically taken from Scrooge in similar fashion as was his mother. Fan died while giving birth to her only son, Scrooge's nephew, Fred. Fred is portrayed as a happy, genial fellow who is forever trying to reach out to his uncle Scrooge. He begs Scrooge to join him and his fiancée for holiday dinners, parties, and other social events. Yet, Scrooge essentially does to Fred what his father did to him. He completely ignores Fred, as he holds Fred responsible for taking his precious and loving sister from him. Scrooge, probably much like his father, is intensely conflicted about this, however, since Fan's dying wish was that Ebenezer look out for Fred.

There were other tragedies in store for Scrooge as time went by, but one clear effect of his early childhood trauma was to learn not to trust that there was any permanency in life. What you love will be taken from you, and the pain will be unbearable. That is likely the reason Scrooge's protective unconscious led him to become a hoarder of money. He never spent it or shared it because he was unconsciously fearful of "running out" and being deprived of his life's possessions (i.e., the tangible proof that he exists). When viewed from this historical perspective, the character of Ebenezer Scrooge becomes much more sympathetic despite his noxious behavior.

Later in life, Scrooge is presented with an opportunity to evaluate and consider how he has lived his life. The ghost of his former business partner, Jacob Marley, visits Scrooge one Christmas Eve in an effort to save Scrooge from sharing Marley's miserable fate. Marley, because of his uncharitable ways toward other humans during his lifetime, has been consigned to walk the earth as a ghost in heavy chains for all eternity. He tells Scrooge that he is headed for the same miserable doom unless he changes his ways. To abet Scrooge in this endeavor, Marley says he will send three spirits to visit Scrooge that very evening.

The ghost of Christmas Past appears first. He and Scrooge revisit Scrooge's lonely, traumatic past, as well as the suffering the world had historically endured. When Scrooge is returned to his bedchambers, he is certainly moved by the visions he has seen, but he quickly dismisses them, declaring them a "humbug" or a piece of undigested beef. The ghost of Christmas Present visits next, and again Scrooge is saddened by what he sees, but true to form, he is quite glib in his contempt for the suffering of others.

The third and final ghost, however, Scrooge cannot ignore. The ghost of Christmas Yet to Come shows Scrooge his eventual demise. He brings Scrooge to an untended, uncared for, and unvisited grave. Scrooge is made privy to overhearing the townspeople laughing and joking about who will inherit his estate and how much better the world will be without him. Scrooge is faced with the reality that he has lived badly, that his life has meant nothing, that his legacy is one of disdain and derision, and that no one is even remotely saddened by his death. Scrooge is profoundly impacted by this encounter with his own mortality and vows to change his ways and be a better man. True to his word, Scrooge lives out the rest of his days helping all in need, being exceedingly generous, and creating a lasting legacy of loving kindness and admiration. *Though the physicality of death destroys us, the idea of death may save us.* Dickens's words (along with some minor interpretive literary license of my own!) demonstrate how the awareness of mortality, as opposed to the denial of death, can inspire us to live a life of few regrets. *A Christmas Carol* is one of my favorite stories of early childhood trauma, existential angst, and the redemptive power of choosing to examine one's life and assume responsibility for how it will be lived.

There is no one "right" or best way to practice existential therapy. However, my work has been most influenced by the writings and teachings of existential psychotherapist Irvin Yalom, M.D. Over the years, I have spent so much time reading Yalom's work, watching his videos, and speaking with him both in person and via email that I am rather discomfited to admit that there are times when I'm not sure where his words end and mine begin. Given that Yalom's work has been so meaningful and impactful on my thoughts and practice of psychotherapy generally and sex therapy in particular, we should spend a bit of time discussing him and his thoughts about the practice of existential therapy.

Irvin D. Yalom, M.D.[2]

Irvin David Yalom was born in 1931 to Russian Jewish immigrant parents. Raised in and around Washington, D.C., Yalom attended medical school at Boston University and did his psychiatry residency at Johns Hopkins University in Baltimore, Maryland. In 1962, he joined the faculty of the Stanford University School of Medicine and served Stanford in a variety of capacities until his retirement from the university in 1994. Currently, he is professor emeritus of psychiatry at Stanford.

Much of Yalom's life has been dedicated to teaching other and future psychotherapists the principles of existential thought. Grounded in the interpersonal psychotherapy movement, Yalom believes in the power of an in-depth psychotherapy that is engaged with an awareness of the existential givens of life. Interestingly, Yalom would not consider himself an existential psychotherapist per se. That is to say that he does not see existential psychotherapy as a separate, independent, stand-alone school of therapy. Rather, he views the therapist's awareness of existential principles as being applicable to many different schools of psychotherapy thought and is an advocate for the psychotherapist developing an existential "lens" that can be applied to most any form of psychotherapy.

Yalom has often said that while he greatly valued being a psychiatrist and working clinically with patients, his true passion was to be a writer. He began with the expected scientific publications that would lead one to tenure and promotion, but he soon began writing textbooks. His first and most enduring was *The Theory and Practice of Group Psychotherapy*. This book is about to be released in its sixth edition, and it is arguably the gold standard of group psychotherapy texts. Yalom followed this with other textbooks including the groundbreaking *Existential Psychotherapy* (1980), a text that defined for the mental health profession the theory and practice of the existential approach to understanding human suffering and discontent as well as the psychotherapeutic treatment of such maladies.

Yalom always longed to be a writer, but to be more specific, he yearned to write great novels. Given his love of psychiatry and people's stories, as well as his dedication to teaching the next generation of psychotherapists, he set out to write a new genre of novel—the teaching novel. His novels were not only well-crafted stories but narratives that aimed to illustrate the existential struggles of humankind and the path to a life well lived. Novels such as *When Nietzsche Wept* (1992), *Lying on the Couch* (1996), *The Schopenhauer Cure* (2005), and *The Spinoza Problem* (2012) are all wonderfully engaging tales of the tribulations and treatment of a variety of existential conundrums, or to use Yalom's word, existential *givens*. These existential givens are those issues that when confronted, often evoke deep anxiety and distress.

Yalom also wrote highly acclaimed books of psychotherapy tales based on his own clinical work. Using heavily disguised patient descriptions, he produced books such as *Love's Executioner* (1989), *Momma and the Meaning of Life* (1999), and *Creatures of a Day* (2015). In perhaps one of his most widely read books, *The Gift of Therapy: An Open Letter to A New Generation of Therapists and Their Patients* (2002a), Yalom lamented the increasing appeal toward a more medicalized and short-term-focused trend in psychotherapy. Fearing that the most important features of psychotherapy and the psychotherapeutic relationship would be forever lost, he wrote this volume to remind future generations of psychotherapists of the concepts he considered the most significant and powerful in the enactment of psychotherapy.

Yalom has written several other noteworthy books,[3] but the one that impacted me most was *Staring at the Sun: Overcoming the Terror of Death* (2008). Death anxiety is one of the four existential givens Yalom (1980) believes we must confront when determining the nature of the confounding forces in our lives (the others are freedom, isolation, and meaning in life). Death, the experience common to us all, may be the most pervasive existential concern and at the root of all the other givens. For this reason, death and the terror of death will be discussed in detail in a separate chapter. For now, let us turn our attention to an examination of the other three givens.[4]

Freedom

The link between freedom and existential pain is not immediately obvious. After all, who wouldn't desire freedom and all its attendant perks? While freedom certainly does come with many highly desirable advantages, it also comes with the responsibility for how that freedom is to be used. According to Yalom (1980, 2002a), we are, in the deepest sense, responsible for ourselves. Thus, we are ultimately responsible for the design of our lives. We make choices, we act, we fail to act, but there is no abdicating the responsibility for those choices that create much of what we are to become.

Often, patients come to us believing that their troubles lie in something outside of their control. It may be another person or other forces around them. We see this in couples' therapy, particularly when one spouse blames the other for their upset and distress. Even those in individual therapy will complain that their problems are because of their boss's behavior, their friend's behavior, or some other factor over which they have little or no control. While it is certainly true that forces beyond our control can profoundly influence our existence, it is only ourselves that we can control. True, we can have some influence over how others treat us or how our environment is structured, but that control will always be limited, as we don't have the luxury or the power to demand that everyone and everything go according to our wants and desires. The existential psychotherapist tries to get the patient(s) to understand that in order to experience a significant and impactful therapeutic outcome, he/she/they must be willing to acknowledge and assume the responsibility for the decision to make changes. As Yalom has often said to patients, even if 99% of what is hurting you is someone else's fault, we need to look at the other 1%. That is the part that is your responsibility.

Some may say that that is a rather harsh position to take. After all, is it fair to "blame the victim"? Yalom and other existential therapists would say that laying blame is not the intent of such a statement. The aim of such a declaration is to encourage the patient to assume responsibility for the choices they make. So long as the patient concentrates his/her/their attention on the actions of others as the focus of change, the therapist can only offer soothing phrases, colorless coping mechanisms, and commiserating comments. It is only when people assume some measure of responsibility for their own life situation that they can begin to see themselves as having the power to make changes and improve their satisfaction with life.

Unfortunately, patients often resist assuming responsibility for their dis-ease and struggle to make the decisions necessary for change. Frequently, they will look to the therapist to make the decisions for them. While often tempting, it is imperative that the therapist not fall prey to this trap. Not only are our decisions about how people should live their lives often erroneous and misplaced, but offering such direct guidance is antithetical to the therapeutic aims of existential psychotherapy. While we as therapists need to assist our patients in examining the barriers to accepting responsibility for their lives, the patient must be the one to accept the risk and responsibility for making a choice.

Making choices is, however, extremely frightening for some. We have all encountered patients who resist assuming responsibility and making the hard choices in their lives for reasons of guilt for hurting others, fear of making an "incorrect" choice, or a past in which they may have been severely punished for attempts at asserting their own autonomy. They may have been raised by caregivers who taught them to view the world as a dangerous place and that it is safer to be a "reactor" than it is to be an "actor." Regardless of the reason, those who consult with us have often done so because of their frustration and/or unhappiness with their position in life and find themselves frozen in fear, ambivalence, and avoidance. Many of our patients long for certainty in their decision-making and proclaim that they are waiting for the path to be "clear" before taking any action. Too often, they wait for a decision to be made by someone else, an environmental change in their circumstances, or even a sign from God. In essence, they assume an extremely passive approach to the design of their lives.

There are also those who resist the responsibility for freedom of choice because their current situation serves some unconscious need or desire. For example, we have all seen those who verbally proclaim a desire for change and seem to eagerly accept therapeutic suggestions. However, week after week, they return for their psychotherapy session having done none of what they pledged to do the week before. While this can be extremely frustrating for both patient and therapist, the existential psychotherapist will understand this lack of movement as an activation of an existential conflict. Recall that existential psychotherapy focuses on issues related to one's *existence* and those factors that are perceived to threaten such existence. Many of our resistant patients may consciously want to change and intellectually recognize that change will only occur if they are the agent of that change. However, on an unconscious level (the protective unconscious), they may fear autonomy and freedom because they long to be nurtured, protected, and cared for. They are searching for the love and security they may never before have had, and the idea of being free to fend for themselves and make important life choices may feel threatening to their very existence. Let's consider two cases in which the existential issue of freedom and avoidance of responsibility are paramount.

The Case of Shelly and Herb

Shelly and Herb came to see me for frustrations in their marriage of 7 years. Both were in their mid-40s, were in good health, and were highly educated and gainfully employed. This was a second marriage for Shelly, and the first for Herb. The couple had no children.

At our first meeting, Shelly and Herb presented as is typical of many couples I've seen. Shelly complained about Herb's behavior, and Herb complained about Shelly's. In the past 3 years, they had consulted with

four other couples' therapists, none of whom were able to offer any helpful assistance. After several years of stagnation, fighting, and ineffective
couples' therapy, they reported being no further along in the resolution of their marital unhappiness. I had asked them why they thought
they had made so little progress toward improving their marital situation, and I received the answer I was dreading: "Our previous therapists
didn't know what they were doing." Fearing I was destined to be the next
"incompetent" therapist, I asked them about their prior therapies and
what was helpful or unhelpful. Their previous therapists (two of whom
I knew and respected highly) had made several suggestions for behavioral change, improved communication, and increased engagement with
each other. Both Shelly and Herb found these interventions to be foolish
and sophomoric, and they never even tried any of them. I thought this
case had disaster written all over it and wasn't at all looking forward to
working with them. However, I reminded myself that despite their lack
of movement and continued frustration, they were not giving up the
quest to find some help. I agreed to work with them but knew that my
approach had to be substantially different from their prior attempts at
psychotherapy.

Thinking that I might not have a lot of time to work with them, I
decided to be unusually bold in my approach. I began by saying that I
understood they were both very unsatisfied and discouraged. I also said
that since I was the fourth couples' therapist they had seen, I wouldn't
waste any time and would cut to the chase. Even though we hadn't developed a strong therapeutic bond, I began with a challenge (ordinarily not
a good idea!). I put to them that I admired their persistence, but if they
have been so unhappy for such a long time and had refused to even try
any of the prior therapeutic suggestions, are they sure they really want
to stay together as a couple? As I expected, they quickly answered with a
resounding "YES! Why else would we be here?" I then followed by asking them, "Okay, great. Tell me what it is about your relationship that you
value and want to keep together." Shelly and Herb stammered a bit and
then produced some vague, anodyne, nonspecific answers. Our sessions
continued for several months, and each time, I was sure to confront them
with the same essential question, "What is it about your relationship that
is satisfying to you? Can you be more specific about what it is that you
value in each other and your marriage?" Shelly and Herb's answers never

became any more refined or genuine. As their psychotherapist, I found working with them to be often tedious, unsatisfying, and frustrating. I assumed they probably related to me much in the same way they related to each other. Not surprisingly, they weren't disposed to respond to my exhortations that if they wanted to end the stagnation, they would have to be willing to assume the responsibility for making the choices necessary to make changes. Therefore, I vowed to continue my efforts to get them to see the futility of waiting and hoping for "magic."

Eventually, I noticed some cracks in Herb's posture. He seemed to be less resistant to discussing deeper issues during sessions, and he eventually was able to say that he really didn't want to continue in this marriage, that he thought they had married too quickly, and he found few areas of compatibility with Shelly. Shelly, with a look of great surprise, asked Herb if he truly felt that way. Herb replied that while he loved Shelly, he really didn't want to have a life with her and was secretly hoping that she would tire of his stubbornness and lack of movement and would ultimately make the decision to end the marriage. Shelly then sheepishly said that she was hoping for the same. She, too, was very unhappy and didn't think they were well matched as life partners. However, she had already been divorced once and was embarrassed to be divorced for a second time. She felt like a "marital failure" and couldn't bring herself to end the marriage. She had hoped that Herb would grow weary of their situation and initiate divorce proceedings. That way, she could deny that she had made a poor choice in marrying Herb and lay the responsibility for the marriage's failure at his feet.

As can be seen from this illustration, both Shelly and Herb were fearful of admitting what they both knew but didn't want to assume responsibility for. Both seemed to rely on a particularly ineffective strategy . . . hope. Hope that the other would make the decision for them. Hope that by some magical intervention, they would be able to avoid the responsibility for the design of their lives. The late psychiatrist David Viscott was a marked critic of the reliance on hope. In his book *Emotional Resilience: Simple Truths for Dealing with the Unfinished Business of Your Past* (Viscott, 1996), he opines:

> Hope interferes with the natural healing process by leading you to expect to be saved and thus to postpone saving yourself.

When you have hope, you're really in denial. You are insisting: things aren't as bad as they seem; things will get better, the other person will change or will love you again someday. You should accept the truth as soon as possible and make adjustments.

Typically, you count on hope when you are most afraid. You are going to have to face the loss or danger by yourself anyway—why lose time hoping for things to get better while they only get worse?

Hope is a reflection of powerlessness, a child's cry for its mother to deliver him in the face of the fearful unknown.

Hope has destroyed more lives than any other emotion, by thwarting the normal instinct to save yourself.

Hope keeps you from growing.

Give up hope.

The way things are is the way things are.

Unless you do something, nothing is going to change.

Instead of hoping, believe in yourself and act.

(p. 63)

Viscott's words hit hard and challenge a common assumption. That is, most of us believe that hope is a good thing—one should never give up hope. Viscott admonishes us to not rely on a fanciful concept such as hope. American bioethicist Eric Cassell (2004) counters this notion in his book, The Nature of Suffering, by suggesting that "Intense unhappiness results from a loss of that future—the future of the individual person, of children, and of other loved ones, It is in this dimension of existence that hope dwells. Hope is one of the necessary traits of a successful life" (p. 138). Similarly, Sherwin Nuland (1993), in his powerfully influential book, How We Die: Reflections on Life's Final Chapter, advocates for the retention of hope. While Viscott's words may seem harsh, his outlook and belief in the power of people to make changes in their lives is intensely optimistic. My read of both Cassell and Nuland suggests that their version of hope is of a different variety than is Viscott's. Viscott objects to the view of hope as a magical cure that happens by releasing one's own responsibility for life to an unknown dreamlike force. He admonishes us to believe in ourselves and act. In this regard, he echoes the sentiments of Cassell, Nuland, Yalom, and the existential psychotherapist. Let's turn to another case illustration.

The Case of Martin

Martin was a 37-year-old single man who came to see me for "anger management." Martin revealed that he had become increasingly angry as the years had gone by and currently found himself in trouble both at work and with his girlfriend, Lucy.

My early sessions with Martin were pleasant and informative. He told me about his background and his present struggles. Nevertheless, I felt some distance from him. I experienced him as holding back, but I couldn't put my finger on why I sensed that or what the issue could be. After many months, Martin revealed to me that he believed he was transgender. He recalled feeling this disconnect between his internal and anatomical worlds for as long as he could remember but feared revealing himself to anyone. He was sure his family would be disappointed, if not rejecting. He had the same concerns about his friends, co-workers, and Lucy. Martin believed that the recent death of a childhood friend made him face the reality that life was moving on, and his time on earth was temporary. He struggled with an increasing sense that he should follow his heart and explore transitioning, but he swallowed his feelings and tried to push them aside. As a result, his anger had escalated as he felt increasingly conflicted about his life path.

Eventually, after about 2 years of psychotherapy, he decided he needed to tell those closest to him who he believed his authentic, genuine self to be. Naturally, Martin was terrified, but his parents and Lucy were both very supportive (and not particularly surprised by his revelation). Still, whenever he would speak with them, they would ask him innumerable questions. "Are you sure this is what you want?" "Are you sure you're not moving too fast?" "Have you considered all of the implications of this decision?" Martin feared that although his parents and Lucy expressed love and support for him, they were really not pleased with his desire to explore the transition process. He feared disappointing them, and as a result, he would waffle on his decision. Every time he would decide to abandon the exploration of transition, his intense anger would return, and he would lash out at others. Martin wished he could get an unequivocal go-ahead from others, and he begged me to tell him what to do. However, Martin needed to assume the responsibility he was granted as part of being a free person, and this was a decision only he could make and be accountable for. As of this writing, Martin is still struggling, but he recognizes he is happiest when planning for transition. He knows he must be the final arbiter of his decisions and that he is responsible for designing how his life will proceed.

As these case vignettes illustrate, freedom is much more difficult a concept than we may have realized. Many patients fear freedom because it requires the assumption of responsibility for the difficult decisions of creating a life. While there are those who welcome such challenges and responsibilities, many of those who consult with us are fearful, tentative, and avoidant of such obligation and accountability. They fear that taking charge of their own life will lead to calamity and catastrophe. The crux of the avoidance is that those who abdicate responsibility for their life often see this expectation as a threat to their existence.

Let us turn to yet another of Yalom's existential givens that pose a perceived danger to our existence.

Isolation

Yalom (1980) identifies three types of isolation: interpersonal, intrapersonal, and existential. The first two are commonly identified by most psychotherapists. Interpersonal isolation refers to the sense of loneliness that occurs when we are isolated from others. Those suffering from interpersonal isolation will often complain of having no friends, companions, or family members that they feel close to. This can be contrasted with intrapersonal isolation in which one often "isolates" parts of the self from the whole. In this situation, the person often feels out of touch or "dissociated" from their own personhood. We will look more closely at this form of isolation n the chapter on existential sex therapy.

Existential isolation implies the most basic of all forms of isolation, the awareness that no matter how close or connected we may be to others, there is an "unbridgeable gulf" between us and any other human being. Ultimately, we will die; no one can share or take that experience from us. We are responsible for our lives and the choices we make, and we can pin that responsibility on no one else. The fact that we are ultimately alone in the existential dilemmas of life raises tremendous anxiety in many of us, and for some, the awareness of our ultimate aloneness is unbearable.

Yalom (1980) believes that the key to living well with our existential angst is found in the quality of the relationships we have with others. While no relationship can eliminate existential isolation, he is of the opinion that if we are able to acknowledge and confront our ultimate existential isolation, we will be better equipped to lovingly turn toward others and engage in relationships that are connected, fulfilling, and authentic. Once we are able to recognize that we are all creatures who will face an existential aloneness, we can avoid the denial of our definitive and final reality and share in the existential connectedness with those around us.

One presentation of existential aloneness that I have seen often in my practice is that of the "parentified child." The parentified child is one who has experienced a particular form of childhood trauma, the trauma of having to "mature" too quickly. Several of the patients I've worked with felt pressed into caring for a parent who may have been mentally ill, physically disabled, heavily involved in illicit drug use, or experiencing debilitating grief. As a result, these people spend their lives trying to anticipate their nonfunctional parent's every need. They become so focused on pleasing their ailing parent or caretaker that they lose touch with their own emotional needs, so much so that they do not even recognize that they have any needs. In couples' therapy, these are often the partners who always say, "whatever you would like" to their partner's queries about what would they like to do, where would they like to go, what would they like to eat, etc. At first glance, this might look like the ideal life mate, but most quickly tire of this constant acquiescence and feel burdened by having to make all the relationship decisions. They often feel as if their partner is disengaged and disinterested in the health of the relationship. In truth, the giving partner often truly does not know what they want. They are concerned only with pleasing their partner and meeting their partner's needs. Eventually, their partner's need for emotional connection is left unfulfilled, and relationship struggles become inevitable. Consider the following case.

The Case of Janet and Ernie

Janet and Ernie came to see me for problems in their marriage. Both were in their early 60s, and this was a second marriage for both. Janet had been widowed for approximately 15 years, and Ernie had been divorced for approximately one month before meeting Janet.

Janet and Ernie's relationship proceeded quickly. Janet, who was quite independent and successful in her career, longed for the companionship a relationship would provide. Ernie, whose wife initiated divorce proceedings, was frightened and unhappy about the prospect of being alone and was eager to find a new mate as soon as possible. As a result, Ernie pursued Janet aggressively. He was exceedingly solicitous of Janet and did all he could to please her. She described him wonderfully chivalrous, considerate, and polite. He would open doors for her, ask her what she would like to do on dates, and was respectful of her wishes. There was also a palpable sexual chemistry between them, and it felt like a whirlwind romance. After dating for less than 3 months, Ernie asked Janet to marry him. She was hesitant since they had known each other for such a short time but was taken with him and decided to make a leap and "throw caution to the wind."

The first few months of marriage were enjoyable for both. However, over time, Janet became less enamored of Ernie's constant acquiescence to all her desires. Indeed, whenever Janet asked Ernie what he wanted, he demurred, saying, "Whatever you would like, my dear." Janet came to realize that Ernie never expressed a preference for anything, never made any plans, and never took the initiative for anything in their relationship unless she asked him to. Janet began to have doubts about the relationship and felt burdened by having to make all the decisions. Ernie was distressed by Janet's unhappiness and was perplexed why any woman would be dissatisfied with a partner who gladly caters to their every whim. They began to bicker frequently and, after approximately 2 years of marriage, decided to seek consultation.

As I got to know them, parts of Ernie's history seemed especially relevant. Ernie revealed that this was the primary reason his first wife had divorced him. She, too, found him to be a "nonpartner" in the relationship and felt their marriage had stagnated. He was confounded as to why she found his "love for her" to be wanting, and he was particularly fearful that Janet was considering leaving him as well.

Ernie disclosed that as a child, he felt as if he was responsible for his mother's emotional well-being. Ernie had a younger sister who died from a rare birth defect at 4 years of age. Soon after his sister's death, Ernie's parents began fighting. Ernie's mother plunged into a deep depression, and his father eventually left the family. Ernie recalls being terrified that his mother would disappear, as did his sister and father, and became exquisitely tuned in to his mother's emotional state. If she was sad, he tried to cheer her up. If she cried, he would hug and hold her. In essence, he vowed to do everything in his power to meet her every need. As a result, Ernie grew up never considering his own needs, wants, or desires. Ernie was unaware that he might even have any requirements or yearnings of his own. When he married his first wife, he insisted his mother live with them so that he could take care of her and be sure she did not feel abandoned. For quite some time, Ernie happily attended to both his mother and his wife until his mother died after he had been married for approximately 10 years. Ernie recalled being surprised that the death of his mother did not bring him much sadness. While he certainly loved her and would miss her, he found himself experiencing a strange sense of relief. Ernie was perplexed by this yet didn't spend any energy examining his feelings. Rather, he plunged himself into serving his wife until she "blindsided" him by filing for divorce.

The case of Janet and Ernie shows the relational problems that are bound to manifest if one partner suffers an existential isolation from the self. Even though on the surface, Ernie looks like a highly relational being, his isolation from himself interferes with his ability to bring much of himself to the relationship. As a result, he is perceived as a poor relationship partner for someone who is looking for deep intimacy and connection. Men like Ernie are often seen as rather vacuous, even though they are extremely giving and attentive. Ernie never was able to understand the importance of building his own life and personhood, and it wasn't until he agreed to begin individual therapy that he began to separate from others and develop an independent voice.

The final given we will examine in this chapter is meaning. We will then move to the next chapter and examine the final and most powerful (and often dreaded) topic—mortality and the terror of death.

Meaning

The search for meaning is a common reason for seeking psychotherapy. As a psychotherapist, many times, I have encountered patients who express concerns such as: "My life feels so empty," "I am so bored with my life," "I feel as if I have no purpose," "Nothing seems to matter any-more," or "I have no idea why I was put on this earth?" Routledge (2018) has suggested that the recent increase in suicides in the United States is in large part related to an overwhelming crisis of meaninglessness. Yalom (1999, 2002a) has suggested that humans are meaning-seeking creatures who struggle to imbue their life with meaning while living in a world devoid of any intrinsic meaning. The awareness of the temporariness of our existence leads some to question, "What is the point?" when all will ultimately end and disappear.

The problem for many patients (and many therapists) is the mistaken assumption that meaning in life can be easily identified and be pursued directly. In this regard, meaning is much like sleep, sexual arousal, and happiness. The more these states are pursued directly, the more elusive they become. Have you ever tried to make yourself fall asleep? Have you ever tried to will an erection? Have you ever thought, "If I only had that (fill in the blank), I would then be happy?" Most all of us have experienced situations such as this only to discover that the more we try to achieve these states, the more we will be frustrated in our attempts to achieve them. I have often heard people say, "Pursue what you love" as if the idea of pursuing one's passion will lead to a life of fulfillment and meaning. Unfortunately, this is a bit of a trap. While pursuing one's passion may lead to a long period of great enjoyment, passions fade. As we age, evolve, mature, and experience new practices, our passion for something will likely wane and again leave us devoid of meaning. How, then, are we humans to make our lives meaningful in a sustained manner?

Yalom (1980, 2002a, 2008) and other existential psychotherapists have suggested that our engagement in human relationships is likely the most potent source of meaning we can know. Strong, connected, genuine, and authentic human engagement will not eliminate the other existential givens, but it will make them matter less. It will reduce our existential anxiety about those insidious threats to our existence. Patients presenting with a crisis in meaning are often those who benefit most from an authentic, engaged therapeutic relationship. The power of the here-and-now focus in a deeply connected psychotherapy will greatly assist our patients in improving the genuineness of their relationships outside of the consultation room.

Consider the following case vignette.

The Case of Roger

Roger came to see me with the complaint of boredom, aimlessness, and depression. Roger was a 61-year-old, recently retired man who was forced out by his company. Roger had been a highly compensated corporate executive who was "asked" to step down from his powerful role in running a large, profitable company. Roger had been with the company for over 30 years, having worked his way up the corporate ladder to his most recent position. He loved his work, especially the fast-paced, high-pressure world of New York City corporate life.

Roger recognized that he was a victim of the corporate world's desire to make way for younger, innovative, cutting-edge leadership minds, and he was given an extremely generous severance package. The company had ensured that Roger would have no financial concerns for the rest of his days.

While Roger agreed to his separation settlement, he did so with great ambivalence. His work had been his life. He had been married to a similarly ambitious, high-powered woman for over 35 years, and the couple had placed career above family and thus had long ago chosen to not have children. Roger's wife was nowhere near ready to retire, and Roger was unsure as to what lay ahead.

Roger reported that he was always fascinated by the real estate market and thought he would begin by earning his real estate license. However, Roger quickly found out that just because he was interested in real estate, it did not necessarily translate into the enjoyment of selling real estate as a career. Indeed, Roger's biggest complaint was that his clients "treat him like a real estate agent!" After having a major role in the running of a large corporation and having employees defer to him as if he were corporate royalty, he found himself less than enthused about being treated like a "regular working Joe." After months of finding his days tedious, uninteresting, and uninspiring, he contacted me at the suggestion of his primary-care physician.

As I came to learn more about Roger, he appeared more and more like a lost, lonely man whose life was bereft of meaning after leaving his job. His wife was occupied with her work, he had no children who would enjoy his help or company, and because he was for so many years immersed in his work, he had never devoted much time or energy to the development of hobbies or friendships. As a result, Roger's days were mostly spent in isolation and consisted predominantly of watching television and walking through shopping malls.

Therapy with Roger was very successful, and he eventually began to cultivate non–work-related friendships. He reported getting a great deal of satisfaction from his new life and credited his psychotherapy and his enjoyment of the feeling of close connection with me with showing him that there were meaningful ways to interact with others beyond the superficiality of work-based acquaintances. Eventually, his wife decided to leave her work as well, and they relocated to a new community, where they became very actively involved in the social and relational aspects of neighborhood living.

The Ghost of Christmas Yet to Come . . .

In this chapter, we have explored some of the most important foundational aspects of existential psychotherapy and the work of Irvin Yalom, M.D. We have examined three of the four existential givens identified by Yalom: freedom, isolation, and meaning. It is now time to examine Yalom's fourth existential given, the one that awaits us all. We now turn to an examination of death and death terror.

Notes

1. For a more complete description of the fundamental tenets of existential psychotherapy, please see Appendix I.
2. For a comprehensive look at Dr. Yalom's life, please see his memoir, *Becoming Myself: A Psychiatrist's Memoir* (2017), New York: Basic Books.
3. For a fascinating and comprehensive literary analysis and discussion of each of Yalom's books, see Jeffrey Berman's *Writing the Talking Cure: Irvin D. Yalom and the Literature of Psychotherapy.*
4. For a comprehensive examination of Yalom's existential givens, please see his textbook *Existential Psychotherapy* (1980).

3

DEATH

The Unavoidable Condition

Death is destiny, as Yalom reminds us in his book *Staring at the Sun: Overcoming the Terror of Death* (2008), and the ensuing fear of death is a universal phenomenon. It used to be said that there are only two things in life that cannot be avoided: death and taxes. Well, it turns out that if you are clever enough, taxes can, indeed, be avoided. Death, however, has yet to meet its match. For many, death is inconceivable, an end we can witness but cannot know (Sale, 2021). It represents the opposite of possibility and the end of our existence as we know it. However, the fact that we will die one day is the one great certainty in life. Becker (1997) suggests that while we may, on a conscious level, acknowledge the reality that we will all die someday and profess that we do not concern ourselves with this actuality, such verbalizations are purely intellectualizations. The affect of fear may be repressed, but the awareness of death must be present behind all of our functioning in order for the organism to be motivated toward the preservation of the self and one's very existence.

DOI: 10.4324/9781003127871-4

Like most psychic defenses, anxiety is helpful for many, as it encourages us to be alert to threats to our existence and to take necessary steps to protect and enhance our lives. As the story of Ebenezer Scrooge illustrates, the fear of death can also be a potent motivator for living our lives in a meaningful and fulfilling manner, one that minimizes regret and despair. In more modern versions, Nora Seed in Matt Haig's (2020) *The Midnight Library* has lived a life of regret and, when confronted with her own mortality via her consideration of suicide, is given the opportunity to revisit many of her life decisions. As a result, she is inspired to discover a better way to live. She discovers what Anna Sale (2021) has described as death's ultimate challenge: to use our time well and with intention. Indeed, much of existential psychotherapy is focused on the future, as it is through the increasing awareness of our eventual fate (i.e., death) that we are able to place greater value on the preciousness of our present and the time we have going forward. Yalom (2002b) reminds us that those individuals who feel they have lived their lives richly have fulfilled their potential and their destiny, experience less panic in the face of death. However, those who have not lived well and are plagued with strong fears of death and their own mortality, perhaps better referred to as "death terror," often find themselves experiencing dysphoria and behaving problematically. As we will see later in this chapter, this dysphoria will manifest itself for many men through messages sent via their penis.

There is a scene in the film *Hannah and Her Sisters* (Allen, 1986) in which Woody Allen, playing the hypochondriacal Mickey, is certain that he is about to learn that he has a terminal illness. He imagines his doctor coming into the room, delivering the devastating news, and leaving him to die a painful, lonely death. When his doctor actually does enter the room and gives Mickey a clean bill of health (again!), he runs from the hospital building, leaping and shouting with relief and joy. Suddenly, he stops on the sidewalk as he realizes that he has been given a reprieve from death for today and probably tomorrow, but eventually, death will catch him. As he is relating his experience to his colleague, Gail, she asks, "You're just realizing this now?" Mickey replies, "Well, I don't realize it now, I know it all the time, but, but I manage to stick it in the back of my mind." Mickey's comments remind us of Becker's (1997) and Solomon's (2019) assertion that while the fear of death may not be readily apparent, and it may manifest itself in a variety of indirect ways, it is ever-present and lies underneath all concerns. Similarly, Yalom (2002b) notes:

> *Death haunts us as nothing else; we've been preoccupied with its dark presence, often just at the rim of consciousness, since early childhood and we have erected denial-based defenses against death anxiety that play a major role in character formation.*

(p. 313)

Most of us, most of the time, can contain our death fears and anxieties and are able to manage them in such a manner that they do not create daily havoc. But there are others of us who are unable to defend themselves from their fears of death, and those fears are terrifying and ubiquitous.

Today, we are witness to a rich illustration of the complexity of dealing with anxiety/terror about death. The world is in the midst of a frightening pandemic. A coronavirus, COVID-19, has spread throughout the world at an alarming rate. As of this writing, we have seen over 111 million cases and more than 2.4 million deaths worldwide. In the United States alone, there have been over 34 million confirmed cases and over one million deaths (*The New York Times*, July 5, 2022). Businesses have shuttered, many people have lost their jobs, and the toll of social isolation from friends and families cannot be calculated. Despite the fact that a vaccination program is well underway, this is a time of crisis and high anxiety. People are concerned for their own well-being, as well as the well-being of those around them. The experience of death anxiety in such circumstances would seem understandable and appropriate, and most have dealt with this pandemic in a reasonably responsible and efficient manner. Social distancing, frequent hand washing, wearing a face covering, etc. have all been shown to be effective in reducing the spread of the virus. However, others have reacted with sheer panic in the face of a terrorizing menace and a threat to their existence. Most of those experiencing death terror, as opposed to death anxiety, have fallen into two distinct camps: those who react with death panic and those who react with death denial.

Those who are experiencing death panic/terror have taken to barely leaving their house. They have everything delivered to their door, including groceries, and fear contamination from all surfaces, leaving packages outside for days before taking them in, touching mail only with gloves, and becoming near agoraphobic. This, despite the scientific reality that the virus is extremely unlikely to be passed on from such contact. Of course, caution is generally a good strategy, but we are seeing some who live with such anxiety that they are glued to their televisions and computers, watching the death count rise. They can't sleep, eat poorly, feel isolated and lonely, and have substantially increased their intake of alcoholic beverages.

At the other end of the spectrum are the death deniers. The death deniers refuse to accept the fact that an often serious and potentially deadly virus has created a significant health crisis in the world. These people refuse to wear masks and often become violent if pushed to wear one when in the presence of others. They will not socially distance and insist that the so-called pandemic is some type of conspiracy, or "fake news" designed to bring down the United States. Despite overwhelming evidence, they refuse to acknowledge the existence of this grave health threat. This refusal has been interpreted as a political statement by some, suggesting that the followers of former United States President Donald Trump don't wear masks in solidarity with him and his political philosophy. While this is undoubtedly true in some cases, this is not likely to explain the large numbers of those who refuse to acknowledge the seriousness of the COVID-19 threat. It is more likely that many of those refusing to accept the virus as a real threat to their existence are experiencing a form of death terror that defensively protects them from acknowledging their level of fear and anxiety. To take the recommended precautions would require them to acknowledge the reality of a threat to their ongoing fears of mortality and sense of safety and force them to consider and accept the reality that death lies in front of us all. Of course, the irony of such defensiveness is that these death deniers place themselves at a much-increased risk of early death by refusing to take reasonable health precautions. Both camps find themselves in the throes of death terror, but neither is able to recognize it as such.

Of particular interest is something that will be discussed in more detail later in this chapter and again in Chapter 5: the pandemic has seen an increase in sexual fantasies, pornography consumption, and solitary sexual activity (Cascalheira et al., 2021). While this may seem to be a benign finding, as we explore the relationship between death terror and sexual behavior, it raises the strong possibility that the significance of these sexual increases is much more profound than we may initially realize.

Even Healthcare Professionals Can
Have Death Anxiety

Death and its impact, while universal concerns, is often underappreciated in the healthcare arena. As a sex therapist, I have often noticed how reluctant many healthcare professionals are to discuss sex with their patients. As an existential psychotherapist, I have noticed how reluctant many healthcare professionals, including psychotherapists, are to discuss death with their patients. Perhaps this should not be such a surprise. Death is difficult to discuss, as its mere awareness is frightening to many. While scores of healthcare professionals see themselves as above the fray of death (a form of death denial to be sure!), none of us is immune to the eventual clutches of the grim reaper.

I recall that after giving my first presentation on the impact of death anxiety on sexual behavior, I received a rather modest round of applause. It was at an annual meeting of the Society for Sex Therapy and Research (SSTAR), and I fully expected an enthusiastic response to my presentation. I was puzzled as to why my presentation didn't arouse more of a reaction or provoke many probing questions. I was left to think that perhaps the presentation that I found so riveting and thought-provoking was nothing more than a curiosity and a reflection of the banal. However, the next day, several of my colleagues stopped me in the hallways of the conference center to chat about my talk. I vividly recall one of my most cherished colleagues commenting to me, "I'm not sure what I think of your theory, but I didn't sleep all night!" It was then that I realized that I had likely provoked the exact anxiety in much of my audience that I had been lecturing about. Merely introducing the topic of death, even to a group of seasoned healthcare professionals, will increase the awareness of the inevitability of death's presence and will often create an underlying level of anxiety that many wish to stifle and ignore.

Danielle Ofri (2019), the noted internist and physician-writer, recently posted an essay describing a patient visit in which the patient suffered a medical emergency during what should have been a routine office visit. This occurrence shook her in a profound way. She was unable to sleep and, for the next 18 hours, found herself in a state of heightened anxiety. As she reflects on this experience, she acknowledges that the fear of death doesn't disappear when you become a doctor. However, most times when a doctor confronts death, he/she is prepared. That is, being called to an event after it has already begun, complications from surgery, a cardiac arrest in a critically ill patient, a seizure in a patient with a seizure disorder, and the like. However, should death appear when one is unprepared, even a physician's defenses are likely to be disordered and unsettled. The veil of death denial cloaked in compartmentalization, euphemistic language, and professional jargon collapses when health-care professionals see and feel death up close and intruding into one's private, protected space. Perhaps it should be little surprise that the topic of death has received scant attention in the healthcare literature. Such is much less the case when considering representations of death and death anxiety in literature, music, and the arts. Great writers and artists have often recognized the impact of mortality and its attendant fears and have been much bolder than many health professionals in acknowledging and appreciating its bearing on the human condition.

Racing With "Father" Time

In *Richard II*, William Shakespeare laments, "I wasted time, and now doth time waste me." The acute awareness of the limited amount of time we have on this earth creates a panic, or death terror, in many men such that they live their lives with an intensity that borders on the obsessive. Of course, this phenomenon is not limited to men, but my experience suggests that such suffering is particularly salient to males. Consider the plight of the "workaholic." A recent *New York Times* article (2021) discusses findings of a recent study by the World Health Organization (WHO). The WHO study estimates that long working hours led to 745,000 deaths worldwide in 2016, a 29% increase over the year 2000, and men accounted for approximately 72% of these fatalities. Furthermore, the study indicates that, particularly in the United States, excessive work hours are not the result of economic need. Indeed, it is the most affluent Americans who work excessively long hours, and many American men appear to take great pride in working hours that are well beyond the limits of what the WHO considers healthy. It would appear that many who work well beyond the bounds of economic necessity do so for some other compelling reason. It is as if these men are expecting, on some level, to "run out of time" before achieving a life of meaningfulness. For these men, the path to evade death is to keep moving and never stop. They live as if they need to keep a step ahead of death as it chases them. As a result, their panicked run from mortality leads to a fanatical and potentially life-threatening compulsion to work as hard as they possibly can and not succumb to leaving this earth with any unlived parts. Poet Dylan Thomas (1957), in the first two stanzas of what may be his best-known poem, "Do Not Go Gentle Into That Good Night," pens the words:

> Do not go gentle into that good night,
> Old age should burn and rave at close of day;
> Rage, rage against the dying of the light.
>
> Though wise men at their end know dark is right
> Because their words had forked no lightning they
> Do not go gentle into that good night.

Thomas recognizes that death is inevitable, but in this ode to his dying father, he beseeches him to rage against death. To fight to live as long and as well as possible. To live until his words had "forked lightning," or left a substantial impact.

Similarly, in Lin-Manuel Miranda's stage version of *Hamilton*, Alexander Hamilton authors papers with an energy and a drive that seems unmatched by any of his peers. This is clearly illustrated in the song "Non-Stop" (Miranda, 2015), which details a conversation between Hamilton and Aaron Burr. Burr says:

> Even though we started at the very same time,
> Alexander Hamilton began to climb.
> How to account for his rise to the top?
> Maaaan, the man is non-stop.

Hamilton later responds with:

> I imagine death so much it feels more like a memory
> When's it gonna get me?
> In my sleep? Seven feet ahead of me?
> If I see it comin', do I run or do I let it be?
> Is it like a beat without a melody?
> See, I never thought I'd live past twenty.
> Where I come from some get half as many.

As anybody why we livin' fast and we laugh, reach for a flask,
We have to make this moment last, that's plenty.

According to Miranda's adaptation, Alexander Hamilton is no stranger to death and loss. He was abandoned by his father shortly after his out-of-wedlock birth, and his mother died when he was a young boy of 12. His notion that he would never live past 20 speaks volumes about his sense that death is always just a step behind, a sentiment characteristic of so many who have experienced early loss. Indeed, one of the prominent features of death anxiety in men is the early loss of a father or other important caretaker figure. Many men who have suffered the early death of their father live under the cloud of a foreboding sense that they will not live beyond the age at which their father died.

While I know little of what drives him, University of Alabama head football coach Nick Saban is remarkably accomplished in his field. With an 87% win record and seven national championships (more than any other college football coach in history), Nick Saban is widely recognized as the GOAT (the greatest of all time). Coach Saban has a reputation for being a tireless worker who allows himself only 24 hours after winning a national championship to enjoy the accomplishment, and then he is on to the next season. He drives his assistants and players with a relentless fervor to be the best they can be—an intensity that is matched only in the way he pushes himself. It is probably not a coincidence that Saban's father, Nick Sr., died suddenly from a massive heart attack at the young age of 46. Coach Saban knows as well as anyone that life can be taken suddenly, early, and capriciously. Much like Alexander Hamilton, Saban labors as if he is afraid of missing out or running out of time. Should I be fortunate enough to have the opportunity to meet him, the impact the precipitous death of his father may have had on his work routine will be one of the first questions I will ask.

In a strikingly poignant album, singer-songwriter Loudon Wainwright III (2012) has an explosion of powerful songs following his passing the age at which his father died. In the liner notes (a much-missed relic from the past!) Wainwright recalls the words of his father writing about his own father:

If I remain still, if I am alone and silent long enough to hear the sound of my own blood or breathing or digestion above the rustling of leaves or the whir of the refrigerator, my father is likely to turn up. He just arrives unbidden in the long running film of my thoughts, like Hitchcock in his pictures, and he looks for all those 40-plus years of disembodiment much like himself, big and sandy haired with freckles on the back of his hands, perhaps a bit more diffident in the way he holds himself than I remember. He doesn't stay long, and as far as I can tell his visits have no message. Yet—even though years of therapy have led me to make the dark whistling claim that he's finally dead and gone—my father, who died when I was 17 continues to be my principal ghost, a lifelong eminence grise, and only my own end will finish it.

And, in the album's title track, he writes:

Older than my old man now.
I wasn't sure this day would come.
I been living underneath his thumb.
But I don't feel so free—I don't even feel like me.
Now that there's no race left to run.
Older than my old man now.
I guess that means I kicked his ass.
But just 'cause you survive
That don't mean you feel alive
And your demise will come to pass.

Wainwright's words are potent illustrations of the haunting sense of being chased by death and how death terror often resides within the essence of many men. For many men who have experienced early loss, especially that of their father, their existence always feels precarious. Wainwright's words also evoke the phenomenon of intergenerational trauma (Atlas, 2022). Wainwright's grandfather died at age 43 when his father was 17. According to Atlas, "every family carries some history of trauma. Every trauma is held within a family and leaves its emotional mark on those who are yet to be born" (p. 3).

Similar sentiments have been expressed by *New York Times* op-ed editor David Belcher (2020) when he reached the age of 56, the age at which his father died. Belcher was a young boy just shy of his 13th birthday when his father, suffering from an excruciatingly painful cancer, was taken from him. In a powerful NYT column, Belcher writes:

Like my father, I've traveled extensively in my life and career, much of it for work but mostly, admittedly, to run. Perhaps to run as my father did . . . I think I am fleeing what my father must have been: the fear of an unfulfilled life, driven by the urgency that it could all be ripped away from me at any moment . . . My aloneness in my travels—and my fear, at this semi-ripe age, that it could all go haywire for me too—is, I suspect, common among grown children whose parents died young. I've sought—and still seek, in the age of 24-hour work cycles, hookup apps and boundless TV ad escapism in every corner of the planet—emotional refuge in all the places that feel safe and immediate. There is not much comfort in the future when it's ripped away from you at a young age.

There are numerous other instances of well-known people expressing similar sentiments related to having been visited by death in early life. New York Yankee great Mickey Mantle, who lived a life of notorious excess, has been quoted as saying, "If I knew I was going to live this long I'd have taken better care of myself" (Roberts & Smith, 2018). Mantle's father died at 39, and Mickey frequently quipped that he doubted he would live past 40. To his surprise, "the Mick" lived to the age of 63. Rod Serling of Twilight Zone fame died at age 50 following a heart attack and open-heart surgery. According to his wife, Serling's father died at 52, and Rod felt this hanging over his head for much of his adult life. Media personality Larry King is reported to have been obsessed with death since childhood. King had a brother who died at 6 years old, and his father died of a massive heart attack when Larry was only 9. According to a recent New York Times article (2021), King spent much of his life dodging death and feeling haunted by its specter. He reportedly took four human growth hormone pills every day, hoping they would buy him more years of life. And the highly accomplished astronaut Chuck Yeager admitted that he was always afraid of dying. Yeager's parents lived relatively long lives, but his sister, Doris Ann, was accidently killed at age 2 by their 6-year-old brother, Roy, who was playing with a loaded shotgun (Yeager, 1985). Yeager was clearly traumatized by being visited by death in early childhood. The tragic death of his sister is likely what propelled Yeager to live as if he was running out of time. The traumatic impact of the early loss of a father and its effect on men's problematic sexual behavior will be more fully explored in Chapter 5.

Quieting Death Terror

While few are unaffected by the limits of mortality, not everyone feels terror at the prospect of eventual certain death. Indeed, as Yalom and others remind us, it is the awareness of death that may inspire us to live our lives well. In addition, those with strong beliefs in an afterlife may also experience less fear related to mortality. However, in psychotherapy, we are most likely to encounter those who do tremble at the thought of nonexistence and find themselves faced with the corporeality of a life inhabited by regret.

In some instances, the words of great philosophers and therapists may mollify the horror of death. Yalom (2008) references the concept of *rippling* as a potential means to palliate the dread of demise. According to Yalom, "rippling refers to the fact that each of us creates—often without our conscious intent or knowledge—concentric circles of influence that may affect others for years, even for generations" (p. 83). While our physical existence ends, our impact on those around us may live on. Some of us may take great comfort if we believe that we have transmitted some useful trait, virtue, or words of wisdom to those we leave behind. However, perhaps the greatest hedge against the terror of death is the power of connection that we foster with others during our time on earth. There is little more potent than the joys of deeply connected relationships with others to substantiate that one has lived well. These rich connections often temper the pain of transiency (Yalom, 2008). Elie Wiesel, who survived the horrors of the Holocaust, has been quoted as saying, "Friendship is my religion. And it's a good religion; one can be a fanatic of friendship, but so what? So you will be an extremist? Then you will simply be an excellent friend!" (Burger, 2018, p. 43). Wiesel also had a strong belief that it is the capacity for profound human connection that heals both individuals and societies. Despite the atrocities he'd been witness to, he retained a conviction that if we could connect with each other, we would live lives of great meaning and create societies characterized by kindness, tolerance, curiosity, and acceptance.

The Relationship Between Death and Sex

Lest we forget this is a book about men and sex, Yalom (1980, 2008) reminds us that the power of sex is often called upon to soothe the terror of death. Sex is a life force and, as such, is often experienced as death defeating. Sex is exciting, stimulating, and generative, while death is banal, still, and final. Sex makes us feel alive and therefore counters fear of death. The potency of sex to ward off the terror of death is not often noted in the psychotherapy texts, but the literary world has often noted this phenomenon. In her book *Sex and Death*, author Stephanie Waxman (2008) writes:

> During the week that Big Tessa faced the decision to undergo a risky bone marrow transplant to thwart the great evil, an aggressive cancer, we took a walk in the desert on the outskirts of Palm Springs. It was early April and scarlet blooms were already popping open on the paddle cactus and the air was filled with the scent of sage. After walking in silence for a while, she stopped, and in her usual frank way, asked my advice: In the face of cancer and the transplant—and in either case and in all probability, in the face of death—what action could she take to affirm life?
>
> The answer came to me in a thunderbolt of absolute certainty and I offered it without hesitation and with great conviction: "Have lots of sex."
>
> It was no doubt naïve of me to think it possible to feel sexual when facing such a battle and such choices. But at the moment it seemed logical that the basic act of procreation was the best antidote to destructive forces.
>
> (p. 79)

Waxman recognizes the emotional connection between facing one's mortality and the desire to be sexual. Her comments to Big Tessa are offered with the seeming assurance that the only way to manage the terror of death is to have lots of sex.

In Woody Allen's award-winning film *Midnight in Paris* (2011), the character playing the role of Ernest Hemingway, who has often referenced sex and death in his writings, has his thoughts echoed in Allen's dialogue when he pronounces:

> I believe that love that is true and real
> creates a respite from death. All cowardice
> comes from not loving, or not loving well, which
> is the same thing. And when the man who is

brave and true looks death squarely in the face,
like some rhino hunters I know, or Belmonte, who
is truly brave, it is because they love with
sufficient passion to push death out of their
minds . . . until it returns, as it does to all
men. And then you must make really good love
again. Think about it.

Hemingway, much like Waxman, also references the power of sex to create a sense of immortality, a hedge against the fear of death. A strikingly similar sentiment is echoed by prolific author Philip Roth in his book *The Dying Animal* (2001) when he writes:

> Sex isn't just friction and shallow fun. Sex is also the revenge on death. Don't forget death. Don't ever forget it. Yes, sex too is limited in its power. I know very well how limited. But tell me, what power is greater?

(p. 69)

In an agonizingly expressive passage, Nobel Prize recipient and Holocaust survivor Elie Wiesel in his book *Night* (1958) observed:

> Freed of normal constraints, some of the young let go of their inhibitions and, under cover of darkness, caressed one another, without any thought of others, alone in the world. The others pretended not to notice.

(p. 23)

Wiesel's observations were made while on the train to the Auschwitz death camp. Riders on the train knew they were headed toward certain death, yet some turned to sex in an effort to assuage their terror in the face of guaranteed demise. Sex is, indeed, often hungered for as an emollient from undeniable impermanence.

And who can forget the scene in the film *Midnight in Paris* (2011) in which, after discovering her husband's extramarital affair, Olympia Dukakis's character presses Danny Aiello's by asking:

OLYMPIA DUKAKIS: Why would a man need more than one woman?
DANNY AIELLO: I don't know. Maybe because he fears death?
OLYMPIA DUKAKIS: That's it. That's the reason!

This scene is particularly noteworthy because in my lectures on sex and death anxiety, this is the reference most often recalled by audience members. Yet they remember little else from the film!

In an especially powerful and revealing memoir, Yalom himself notes in the book he and his wife, Marilyn, co-wrote as they were facing her imminent death from cancer (2021):

> But, now, a new obsession has invaded my thoughts: whenever I relax and try to clear my mind, for instance awaiting sleep after turning out the lights, I am visited by enticing sexual thoughts involving women I've known or seen recently. These images are powerful and persistent. I try to block them, purge them from consciousness, turn my thoughts elsewhere. But, a few minutes later, they reappear and again seize my attention. I am flooded with both desire and shame. I wince at such disloyalty to Marilyn, buried only a few weeks ago.
>
> As I look back over the last few weeks, I've also become aware of a curious (and embarrassing) development: intensified interest in women's breasts, especially sizable breasts . . .
>
> I am unsettled and ashamed of these sexual obsessions. A debate proceeds in my mind. How could I so dishonor myself and my love for Marilyn? Is this really how shallow my love is? But, on the other hand, isn't it my task now to stay alive, to begin a new life?
>
> (pp. 169–170)

Yalom, in his characteristic honest and disarmingly candid manner, shares with his readers his own sexual feelings (and conflicts thereof) he confronts in the face of the death of his beloved wife, Marilyn. He, too, unconsciously turns toward sex as a powerful antidote to the terror of experiencing the death of a loved one up close. Irv's grief is evident and profound, but the death of Marilyn also brings him closer to the unambiguous reality that his own death cannot be far behind.

Why Sex?

As the referenced passages as well as most case examples in this book indicate, sex is often turned to in the face of death and death terror. But the question remains, why sex? Why not alcohol or other drugs?

Certainly, they would mollify fear and anxiety. Or why not hoarding money? This is what Scrooge turned to to deal with his mortality dread. Or gambling? Certainly, gambling would provide a spark of excitement that might make a person feel "alive." The psychological literature indicates that mortality salience increases sexual and nonsexual risk-taking behavior in many adults, particularly those with an external locus of control (Miller & Mulligan, 2002). So what makes sex so significant?

As previously noted, sex is a "life force" and thus often counters the fear of death. In its most basic sense, sex represents procreation and the creation of life and therefore has the power to counter fears of death and mortality with a potency greater than any other authority. However, my clinical experience leads me to propose two additional factors that may shed light on the primacy of sex as a neutralizer of death anxiety. The first relates to proximity. The closer death comes to us, the greater the existential threat to our own existence and the resultant increase in death terror. Sex may represent the ultimate psychological dominion over death, and while drugs, gambling, and other behaviors may be sufficient to control death anxiety under most circumstances, it may be sex that steps in at the point of greatest vulnerability.

Consider the situation that Irv Yalom himself faced. Yalom has often written about his own pervasive sense of death anxiety. Many of his clinical tales, novels, and personal disclosures detail anxiety related to mortality. Yet it is only in his most recent book, *A Matter of Death and Life* (2021), which he co-authored with his beloved wife, Marilyn, and which focused on her impending death did he describe his experience of such strong *sexual* urges and longings that entirely confounded him. It is reasonable to assume that the death of his wife, best friend, and confidant of more than 65 years brought his own death closer to him than he had ever before detected.

In addition to proximity, I propose that the nature of one's early childhood trauma must be considered. In my experience, those men I have worked with who experience sexual difficulties are also those who have been most likely to have suffered *relational* traumas. It seems intuitive that fractured significant relationships in the early years would be easily triggered by seemingly benign and idiosyncratic relational occurrences in the present. Such relational fissures can be manifested in the significant sexual relationships of adulthood if our sense of safety, security, and attachment feels threatened. For those with early relational ruptures, connected relationships in the present may provoke a confrontation with our most poignant sensation of vulnerability. The result is a sexual shutdown that often mystifies the man who presents in our offices.

To appreciate the depth of the penis more fully as a conduit of male emotion and ambivalence, we must first be able to appreciate the particular and unique connection between a man and his penis.

A Man and His Penis: A Love Story (of Sorts)

In the Introduction, I discussed the sentiments of men who had either lost penile functioning or experienced severe genital injury. I described their feelings of despair, humiliation, vulnerability, and brokenness. And of course, we should not forget the letter I received from David, who detailed his sorrow, anguish, and pain regarding the compromised function of his penis that led to frequent and intense suicidal thoughts.

The relationship between a man and his penis is complex and profound. While often trivialized, the functioning of a man's penis has implications that go well beyond sexual prowess. The adequacy of the penis carries with it deep existential significance that is often unappreciated in the sex therapy literature. As previously discussed, Yalom and others have reflected on the power of sex to be life affirming and a potent agonist to the terror of death. For men, the penis is the conduit of that sexuality, and in an existential sense, the functioning of the penis is directly connected to a man's sense of vitality and life-energy. The compromise in penile adequacy is unconsciously equated with loss, torpor, lethargy, and lifelessness. In other words, a flawed penis means a heightened sense of vulnerability, fragility, and ultimately a confrontation with mortality. Do you think this is overstating the case? Perhaps. Some have suggested as much, but my experience of sitting with men for almost 40 years and listening to their torment and sorrow regarding the loss of penile ability tells me otherwise.

Earlier in this book, we briefly discussed the often-painful measures men will go to in order to restore penile functioning. While oral medications may be rather benign, men have historically turned to invasive medical procedures to reverse penile insufficiencies. Vacuum devices, penile injections, urethral suppositories, and surgically implanted penile prostheses have all been popular medical approaches for addressing erectile difficulties. Why would men go to such extremes if not for a deep and sonorous voicing of concerns about the core of their existence? Attributing this solely to a sense of masculine power and sexual ability seems overly mechanical, reductionistic, and disingenuous.

There is a scene in the first episode of season one of the HBO series *The Sopranos* (Chase, 1999), a show that voices many existential themes, that begins with organized-crime boss Tony Soprano consulting psychiatrist Jennifer Melfi, M.D., after experiencing a panic attack. Dr. Melfi questions Tony about the circumstances leading up to his collapse from panic. He describes two ducks landing in his backyard swimming pool and the birth of ducklings. She later asks him if he feels depressed, and he replies, "Since the ducks left . . . I guess." She notes that the ducks leaving was the last thing Tony remembers before losing consciousness and suggests they talk about them. Later in the episode, Tony hesitantly reveals a recent dream to Dr. Melfi in which he describes his belly button as a Phillip's-head screw. He explains that, in his dream, he is working to unscrew his belly button, and once it is unscrewed, his penis falls off. He remembers being in a panic, looking for someone to reattach his penis, when a bird suddenly swoops down, grabs his penis, and then flies away. Dr. Melfi probes Tony to say more about the bird. He recollects it was a type of water bird, and Melfi suggests it may have been a duck. At the mention of the ducks, Tony begins to tear up and laments the loss of the duck family in his yard. Tony then acknowledges that he fears losing his family, just like he lost the ducks, and says the dread of family loss is always with him.

Tony's panic attacks were the result of a great deal of repressed, unacknowledged existential angst. The ducks and ducklings in his backyard triggered the explosion of his unexpressed emotions. His family was slipping away from him. He was dealing with unresolved grief related to the death of his father, a highly conflicted relationship with his mother, concerns about his children and his marriage, and the erosion of his "business family" as the culture of organized crime in America was changing. In essence, Tony saw his very existence slipping away from him, and in his dream, he lost his *penis*. His penis represented vitality, life, and his essential being. From an existential perspective, it is not surprising that such distress was manifested through the guise of his penis. The flying away of the ducks signified for Tony the erosion of his life as he had known it, and the panic attacks were his protective unconscious's attempt to alert him to this existential danger. It would be hard to ignore that the fact of the centrality and function of his penis in this dream were hardly sexual, at least in the ways in which we typically think about men, sex, and their penis.

Perhaps the case for an existential understanding of the penis as a life force and neutralizer of death anxiety can be strengthened by examining another, often confounding, male issue—penis size. Concerns regarding penis size have plagued men for generations. I recently came across an unattributed quote on Facebook that goes something like this:

> It takes 7 seconds for food to pass from the mouth to the stomach. A human hair can hold 3kg. The length of a penis is 3 times the length of the thumb. The femur is as hard as concrete. A woman's heart beats faster than a man's. Women blink twice as much as men do. We use 300 muscles just to keep our balance when we stand. The women have finished reading this message. The men are still looking at their thumbs.

Humorous? Sure. But as is the case with much of what we find humorous, there are elements of truth. Truth be told, I found myself looking at my own thumb before continuing! Many clinicians and sex researchers have observed that most men believe that their penis is too small. Noted sexologists Barry and Emily McCarthy (2021) claim that approximately 80% of men believe that their penis is smaller than average, even though evidence does not support this reality. Other studies (King, 2020) have reported a somewhat lesser number of men with inaccurate perceptions of average penis size, with a range of 45% to 68.3% of men reporting dissatisfaction with the size of their genitalia. Regardless of the exact percentage, it is clear that many men believe that their penis is of inadequate size and wish it were larger. Urologist Aaron Spitz, M.D. (2018), in discussing the men who come to see him with concerns related to penis size, suggests that the vast majority of men with this complaint have a penis that is totally normal in its proportions. He diagnosis them with small penis syndrome, a diagnostic label first coined by Murtagh in 1989. According to Wylie and Eardley (2007), small penis syndrome (SPS) can be defined as "an anxiety about the genitals being observed, directly or indirectly (when clothed), because of concern that the flaccid penis length and/or its girth is less than the normal for an adult male, despite evidence from a clinical examination to counter this" (p. 1449). Pastoor and Gregory (2020) emphasize that SPS is distinct from body dysmorphic disorder (BDD), and they have seen male patients who recognize their penis is of normal size but want it enlarged anyway. Spitz (2018) outlines some of the techniques and procedures sought by men desiring penile enlargement such as penis pumps, penile traction (devices that promote penis enlargement via stretching the penis), jelqing (tightly encircling the shaft of the penis with thumb and finger and milking the penis from base to tip firmly and slowly to squeeze blood forward and stretch out the tissues and vessels), and penis enlargement surgeries. All the mentioned authors avow that regardless of technique, satisfaction rates with efforts to enlarge a man's penis are notably low.

So what are we to make of this phenomenon? How do we explain or understand men's seemingly obsessive concern with penis size? We have already seen that providing information about the reality of average penis size is not impactful. Consistent data abounds on the average dimensions of the penis, and as mentioned by Pastoor and Gregory (2020), even men who acknowledge that their penis is of normal size seek penile-enlargement interventions. Spitz (2018) highlights that it is not partner dissatisfaction that stirs size inadequacy in most men. Indeed, he suggests that in heterosexual relationships, 85% of women report being satisfied with the size of their partner's penis. This sentiment is echoed by University of Florida psychology professor Laurie Mintz, who says in her award-winning 2017 book that of hundreds of women, when asked an open-ended question about what matters most to them during intercourse, not one mentioned penis size!

King (2020) provides a common perception of this concern. He reports that sex researchers have suggested that men equate penis size with sexual competence and masculinity. Certainly, comments about penis size have often been used to insult and demean men. Hemingway (1964) writes of a conversation with F. Scott Fitzgerald in which Fitzgerald reveals that his wife, Zelda, is the only woman he has ever had sex with. He further states that he is fearful of having sex with other women because Zelda told him that the way he was built (i.e., the size of his penis) would never make a woman happy (i.e., sexually satisfied). Hemingway goes on to describe the lengths he went to in order to convince Fitzgerald that his penis was perfectly normal and that Zelda was just being cruel. There is a scene in the film *Notting Hill* in which Julia Roberts, portraying a famous actress, overhears a conversation among a group of men in which they are commenting on her looks and imagined sexual proclivities. Upset at being objectified and depersonalized, she approaches them and tells them they likely have a penis the size of a peanut. Obviously, this retort is meant as an insult, and it leaves the men speechless. Nevertheless, I would suggest that this oft-proffered explanation regarding the significance of penis size does not do justice to the depth and significance of men's concerns about the length and girth of their penis. While it is tempting to accept the simplistic explanation of size equals sexual prowess and masculinity, that seems an underdeveloped and inchoate construal given the intensity and almost universality of the concern.

Viewed through an existential lens, the size of a penis can be conceptualized as an indicator of aliveness, vitality, and immortality. If sex is the life force (i.e., the antidote to death anxiety) and the penis is the conduit of that life force, it would seem conceivable that penis size is psychologically and existentially equated with a hedge against mortality and death. The bigger the penis, the more life affirming it becomes. The notion that men would experience such angst and go to such efforts to improve the functioning and/or the size of their penis for purely sexual reasons represents a superficial and one-dimensional understanding of the sexuality of men. Sexual science has historically trivialized the importance of penile stature and the psychological significance of the penis. It is the aim of existential sex therapy (discussed in the following chapter) to provide a framework for a deeper understanding of the importance of the penis and a more satisfying and complete treatment paradigm.

In this chapter, we have examined the fourth and final of Yalom's existential givens, death. Perhaps living at the core of each of the givens, death represents the greatest challenge to our existence. It is unavoidable yet difficult to accept. Solomon (2019) reminds us that clinical observations and empirical research confirm that death anxiety plays a potent and pervasive role in many psychological maladies.

We have also posited that sex (specifically the functioning of the penis) can be a powerful force in countering fears of mortality. In the next chapter, we will describe a new view of understanding the sexual difficulties of men, existential sex therapy. Existential sex therapy (EST) is an approach to understanding and treating sexual problems based on

Yalom's principles of existential psychotherapy. Let us begin our exploration of EST with an excerpt from a clinical tale of Yalom's from his 2015 book *Creatures of a Day*. Yalom is describing a session with a male patient who is describing a recurrent nightmare that had been visiting him over the last month. Yalom recalls his patient Alvin saying:

> "I'm in the bathroom. I'm looking into the mirror, and suddenly I see a big black bird swooping into the room. I don't know where it's come from or how it's gotten inside. The house lights begin to dim, and then they go off completely. It's pitch black. I'm frightened and run through other rooms, but I hear and feel the flapping wings following me. That's when I wake up frightened, heart pounding, and strangely, with an electric erection." He grinned at the lilt of his alliteration.
>
> I grinned in return. "Electric erection?"
> "It was buzzing, throbbing."
> "What hunches do you have about this dream, Alvin?
>
> (p. 63)

Indeed, Alvin. What hunches do you have about this dream? What is your penis saying to you?

4

EXISTENTIAL SEX THERAPY

Sex therapy is changing. Recent years have seen an unprecedented willingness to incorporate a wide variety of therapeutic interventions into the treatment of sexual problems. According to Meana et al. (2020), the field of sex therapy is increasingly incorporating interventions from therapeutic orientations and modalities as diverse as family systems, emotionally focused therapy, and others. The clinical isolation that once defined sex therapy in the larger landscape of psychotherapy appears to be over. As our understanding of sexuality has evolved, along with a proliferation of books, magazine articles, and the internet, our access to more and often better sex information has been unparalleled. The myriad nuances of sexuality and sexual function have become increasingly pronounced, and the complexity of human sexual behavior is appreciated in ways never imagined in the early days of Masters and Johnson's **Slack Technologies** (NYSE: WORK) Of course, growth is unavoidably complicated and difficult, and many of the recent shifts in our ideas of what constitutes "sex therapy" have been highly controversial and hotly

DOI: 10.4324/9781003127871-5

debated. Nevertheless, we are seeing an evolution in a field that some once described as stagnant (Schover & Leiblum, 1994; Kleinplatz, 2003b).

While existential therapy has been referenced in the sex therapy literature by only a few authors (Watter, 2018; Kleinplatz, 2017; Barker, 2011), I have seen a strong resonance and increasing interest in the topic during my own presentations to professional and lay audiences. During the past 15 years, I have been approached by numerous clinicians asking me to supervise their sex therapy cases so that they may better include an awareness of existential issues in their practice of sex therapy.

There are a few features of existential psychotherapy that make it a particularly good fit for understanding and treating sexual problems, especially those occurring in men. The existential lens is a relational construct. Spinelli (1997) reminds us that existential theory insists on viewing human beings from a relational rather than an isolated perspective. That is, we do not live in a vacuum, and there is little that one does that does not have relational reverberations. Spinelli (1997) further states that much of human suffering is best understood as expressions of conflicts and insecurities that arise from the relational experience, or our interactions with the world in which we live. He suggests:

> Existential-phenomenological theory presents us with a view of human existence that places anxiety at its center. It suggests that our experience of living is never certain, never fully predictable, never secure. Instead, our very embracing of life presents us with all manner of "challenges": challenges to the meanings we have built up and live by, challenges to the aims and purposes with which we imbue our lives, challenges, indeed, to the very continuation of our existence.
>
> (p. 6)

Notice in Spinelli's words the themes of anxiety, uncertainty, and existence. As we shall see throughout this chapter, these themes will resonate strongly through our exploration of the causes and cures of male sexual dysfunction. In addition, Spinelli, much like Yalom, asserts that the relational aspect of existential theory extends to the process of existential therapy. That is, the existential psychotherapist places great importance on the quality of the therapeutic relationship itself, and it is believed that the therapeutic relationship is our most potent tool in the psychotherapy process.

Van Deurzen & Iacovou (2013b) add that existential philosophers recognize the centrality of the relationship to human existence, and they stress the importance of recognizing individuality as secondary to relationships. This philosophy stands in stark contrast to much of what is popular in psychology and psychotherapy today. Much of modern-day psychological thought focuses on the importance of developing the self and assuming little to no responsibility for the impact of behavior on partners or those around us. To be sure, existential psychotherapy also places a considerable emphasis on the development of the individual, but always with a focus on how the way one lives life intersects with the lives of others. In this regard, existential theory assumes a strong Nietzschean view inasmuch as love and relationships can be much improved if we first learn to love ourselves and also to love our lives, taking responsibility for what we make of our lives ourselves rather than holding others responsible for it (van Deurzen & Iacovou, 2013b). Similarly, psychotherapist and Jungian analyst James Hollis declares:

> The best thing we can do for our relationships with others . . . is to render our relationship to ourselves more conscious. This is not a narcissistic activity. In fact, it will prove to be the most loving thing we can do for the Other. The greatest gift to others is our own best selves. Thus, paradoxically, if we are to serve the relationship, we are obliged to affirm our individual journey.
>
> (van Deurzen, 2013)

Existential psychotherapy places great emphasis on the importance of all people assuming responsibility for the way in which they conduct their lives and the belief that it is only once a person can take responsibility for their part in what is going wrong that they can be a vigorous and dynamic force in the process of making it right (van Deurzen, 2013). Those of us who do couples' therapy will readily relate to the phenomenon in which partners come into therapy blaming their unhappiness on their partner. I am reminded of the words of the late satirists James Thurber and E.B. White (1929), who said:

> there is a very good reason why the erotic side of [man] has called forth so much more discussion lately than has his appetite for food. The reason is this: that while the urge to eat is a personal matter which concerns no one but the person hungry, the sex urge

involves for its true expression, another individual. It is this "other individual" that causes all the trouble!

(p. 27)

Stadlen (2013) adds that she finds it often counterproductive to try to solve the couple's practical problems, however urgent. She suggests that the practical problems (symptoms) are often a distraction, and once couples decide to accept responsibility for their actions, they are able to come up with solutions for themselves. In essence, Stadlen is echoing the thoughts of Yalom and others who have suggested that existential psychotherapy focuses on "process" as opposed to "content." This, too, is a theme we will reference often when discussing the existential approach to meeting the myriad problems men face with their sexuality and sexual functioning.

Existential Psychotherapy and Sex Therapy

Many of the seminal precepts of existential sex therapy are not new. However, they have often gone unnoticed in the sex therapy literature. Specifically, the existential psychotherapist looks beyond the presenting symptom and seeks to understand what the symptom is saying. Recall the concept that the "penis speaks." In addition, existential psychotherapy looks to humanize the individual by not reducing his difficulties to arbitrary and limiting labels such as those required in standard psychiatric diagnoses. Unfortunately, this is a battle existential psychotherapists have been fighting for decades. In 1946, existential psychiatrist Viktor Frankl wrote:

For too long a time—for half a century, in fact—psychiatry tried to interpret the human mind merely as a mechanism, and consequently the therapy of mental disease merely in terms of a technique. I believe this dream has been dreamt out. What now begins to loom on the horizon are not the sketches of a psychologized medicine, but rather those of a humanized psychiatry.

A doctor, however, who would still interpret his own role mainly as that of a technician would confess that he sees in his patient nothing more than a machine instead of seeing the human being behind the disease!

(Frankl, 1959, pp. 156–157).

Frankl was clearly overly optimistic in declaring that the dream of technique-focused therapy has been dreamt out, yet he is certainly not a lone voice. Sex therapist Suzanne Iasenza writes in her recent book *Transforming Sexual Narratives: A Relational Approach to Sex Therapy* (2020):

> As my thinking and therapeutic techniques evolved over the years, I stopped approaching sex therapy as a technician who could "repair" the "broken couple, or "fix" the "broken" individual, or get the malfunctioning body parts back to work with medical intervention or behavioral techniques. Likewise, I no longer believed that mere cognitive understanding of erotic desires would change behaviors in the bedroom, although those insights are important.
>
> (p. 9)

Iasenza acknowledges that we've been fighting the battle for a more humanized sex therapy and psychotherapy for quite some time, and that struggle still exists.

While certain techniques are clearly useful and therapeutically helpful, much of sex therapy has been heavily reliant on techniques that are directed at eliminating problematic sexual functioning. Frankl (1952, 1975) has been highly critical of this approach to psychotherapy. He talks of the importance of *dereflection*, the idea that focusing on the symptom actually creates an obstacle to resolution. For example, if you have ever tried to will yourself to sleep, you will have discovered that the more you focus on trying to sleep, the more elusive sleep becomes. This is because sleep is not something that can be directly pursued. Sleep is a by-product of another state, a state in which overfocusing on an outcome pushes the desired result farther from reach. The same could be said for sex and sexual arousal. The more a man's penis is the focus of attention and intervention, the more elusive good sexual functioning becomes. Sexual arousal, much like sleep, cannot be pursued directly because sexual arousal is a by-product of another state of being. Masters and Johnson (1970) and Weiner and Avery-Clark (2017) likely had an awareness of this in promoting and expanding the concept of sensate focus. The primary goal of sensate focus is to deemphasize goal-oriented sexual outcomes while encouraging the pursuit of pleasure. I have recommended sensate focus to many of my patients over the years, with mixed results. In my experience, sensate focus does not effectively address the concept of dereflection, as patients continue to have the idea of moving toward a more direct focus on the genital response. As a result, sensate focus and other standard sex therapy assignments profess an awareness of the importance of dereflection but often fall short. While it would be grossly unfair and reductionistic to assert that technique-focused sex therapy is poor or ineffective treatment or that sex therapists who focus directly on symptom relief are inferior therapists, the fact remains that many patients leave sex therapy without lasting resolution to their presenting problem and underlying distress. It is for these patients that the existential lens could be most helpful. Existential sex therapy believes that the microscope being placed on the presenting symptom is, in itself, limiting, as it suggests that men have sexual problems for easily explainable reasons. That is, attention is directed toward how to treat "erection problems" as opposed to developing an understanding of what a particular man's erection problems represent and what message his penis is trying to send him.

Similarly, Barker and Langdridge (2013) have suggested that:

> One key way in which existential sex therapy would differ from more mainstream approaches would be in its openness to a multiplicity of possible meanings of sexual experiences and practices. Conventional approaches tend to assume universal causes for sexual problems, and focus on addressing these causes. For example, it is commonly assumed that erectile dysfunction results from the possessor of the penis failing to "perform" on one occasion and then becoming anxious in subsequent sexual encounters.
>
> (p. 60)

Barker and Langdridge argue that rather than focus on universal causes for male sexual problems (i.e., performance anxiety), it is important to discover the *meaning* that erectile loss and erectile function have for any given man. They suggest that there is no single reason for sexual dysfunction and every situation must be assessed for its uniqueness and significance as it relates to the individual man sitting in front of us.

Noted sex therapist Peggy Kleinplatz (2017) offers:

> Sex therapists do not generally know much about or show much interest in existential philosophy or psychotherapy. Correspondingly, existential and experience psychotherapists have traditionally shown minimal interest in dealing with sexuality. This strikes me as a pity because the two have always seemed to me a natural fit. I find it enormously helpful when dealing with sexual problems in individual and couple therapy to use an approach focused (1) not only on the symptom but also on its meaning, purpose, and possibly adaptive value; (2) not only on the objective, physical dysfunction, but also on the subjective experience for the man, woman, or couple; (3) not on whether the problem is organic or psychological, but rather on how it is inevitably both—and also relational and psychosocial and socioeconomic; and (4) not only how to fix the problem, but also on how to use it as an entry point for personal and interpersonal growth and, beyond that how to aim for optimal erotic intimacy.
>
> (pp. 218–219)

Kleinplatz provides perhaps the most comprehensive view of existential sex therapy. She recognizes the importance of dealing with not just the presenting symptom but also the meaning that symptom has for the individual/couple suffering from the dysfunction. In addition, she has an appreciation for the importance of the individual's subjective experience of the problem as well as the import of maintaining a focus on the relational aspects of the presenting obstacle. Finally, Kleinplatz places strong emphasis on the value of appreciating the presenting symptom as an entry point for personal and interpersonal growth. Again, the penis speaks. The task of therapy is to help the man decipher what the penis is saying to him.

My personal interest in existential psychotherapy is likely its resonance for my own existential dilemmas. As mentioned earlier in this text, my early training in sex therapy was very much focused on the work of Masters and Johnson and the principles of behavioral therapy and cognitive-behavioral therapy (CBT). While I know that much of my early work was helpful to my patients, I couldn't shake the sense that I was not doing the best work with them that I could. Something felt incomplete to me, and I found myself feeling much like a technician as opposed to a psychotherapist. Again, I know many, many fine sex therapists who utilize CBT and related techniques with great success, but

I found myself becoming bored with the process. My introduction to the work of Irv Yalom and the existentialists made me come alive both in terms of my own life and in my work with patients. I found myself having deeper and more fulfilling conversations with my patients, and I saw the excitement and enthusiasm in many of them as they made new discoveries and fresh understandings of their emotions and behaviors. My sex therapy patients were describing not only better *sexual* function-ing but also better *relational* functioning.

Let us now return to Alvin's dream in Chapter 3. Recall Alvin describ-ing his recent dream to Irv Yalom and Yalom paying particular notice to his referencing his "electric erection." According to Yalom's story, Alvin had been long plagued by fears of death. As a young man, he lost both parents unexpectedly. Following their untimely deaths, Alvin was una-ble to sleep unless he masturbated. Alvin reported that since their deaths, he masturbated every night thereafter. It was the only way he could feel soothed enough to drift off to sleep. Alvin's therapy with Yalom was precipitated by the early death of his younger brother from lung cancer. Alvin's long-standing death anxiety was exacerbated by his realization that he was the only remaining member of his family still alive, and that meant that his would be the next family death. Yalom points out that many who experience substantial death anxiety fear sleep and darkness, as it psychologically sets the stage for death. Alvin's masturbatory habit is described by Yalom as the use of sex to neutralize the fear of his eventual demise. Yalom describes it as the "protective process" that produced his electric erection as symbolic of the power of orgasm as a means of self-soothing in the face of the terror of death.

Alvin and Yalom spent many sessions focusing on Alvin's death terror, but then therapy began to slow. Alvin was feeling better, sleeping bet-ter, and less consumed with overt thoughts about death. Alvin broached the topic of termination. Yalom, however, wasn't sure that it was time to stop. He felt there was more to do but, of course, left that decision to Alvin. Yalom wanted to explore the manner in which Alvin had arranged his life. Alvin was a very personable man with good social skills but had no real intimate relationships in his life. Because he was single, never seriously partnered, Yalom was concerned about Alvin's inchoate rela-tional life. Alvin acknowledged that his relationship with Yalom was probably his most intimate relationship yet appeared uncomfortable and resistant to the notion of exploring this further. Yalom, however, recognized the resistance as an obstacle to overcome, and he gently but persistently chipped away at Alvin's armor. A pivotal point came about when Yalom suggested to Alvin that there was a strong connection between death terror and an unfulfilled life. This resonated strongly with Alvin, and Yalom seized the opening to explore the resistance further. Alvin then revealed:

> I meet a lot of women, and the same thing happens every time. We go out, have dinner, sex is great, we like one another, and then sooner or later, after a few dates, the women come to my house. And then it ends. Once they see my house, I never see them again.

Yalom found this revelation to be a great curiosity and made the bold suggestion that their next session should be at Alvin's house. Alvin struggled with this suggestion for weeks and vacillated between wanting to continue with Irv and wanting to end therapy. Finally, Alvin relented and agreed to meet with Yalom at his home. What Yalom found was the home of a hoarder. Papers everywhere, stacks and stacks of old magazines, newspapers, books, and old x-ray films. Yalom was surprised at what he saw, especially since Alvin always presented as well groomed and cared for and had a reputation for being meticulous at work. Yalom wisely took the time to discuss their therapeutic relationship and how Alvin was feeling about what was taking place. Alvin expressed great shame and embarrassment at exposing to Yalom the way he lived. Yalom feared he might have pressed too hard to get Alvin to allow him into this space, and sure enough, Alvin cancelled his next sessions and ended the treatment. Yalom lamented a therapy bungled and closed Alvin's file with unease.

Yalom had not heard from Alvin until they unexpectedly ran into each other at a funeral. Alvin saw Yalom and approached him with a big smile. At first, Yalom did not recognize Alvin. Alvin looked great, and with him were his two children and lovely wife. Alvin's wife whispered words of thanks to Yalom, saying he was responsible for their marriage and happiness. Yalom's head began to spin as he tried to understand what had happened that produced such an outcome. After all, his last contact with Alvin felt so incomplete, and he felt he had failed Alvin. He asked to meet with Alvin to better understand the reasons for such a life change. Yalom's conversation with Alvin reminded him of one of the most important tenets of existential psychotherapy, namely the power of the therapeutic relationship. Alvin's time with Yalom opened his eyes to the power and importance of an intimate relationship. While he did not feel the desire for additional psychotherapy, he found himself greatly missing his time with Yalom. This encouraged him to consider the possibilities that a more *relational* life could bring, and he decided to hire a housekeeper to help him organize his home and his life, and he was motivated to take the risk of letting someone get closer and take the chance on complete life. He met his wife about a year later and experienced a happiness that he never before thought possible.

I, too, have discovered some of the same psychotherapy mysteries described by Yalom. Like many of us, I have had cases that ended in ways that left me thinking I had made some tremendous error or misstep only to find out years later that my time spent with a given patient was more powerful and life affirming than I realized. To me, this is what makes psychotherapy fascinating. We really never know exactly how it works and often find ourselves having to sit with great uncertainty. Yet time and time again, the psychotherapy process reveals its effectiveness to us.

I believe that much of what creates sexual problems for men is rooted in a triggering of some early childhood relational trauma. Such was the case with Alvin. His fears of death and loss were intricately connected, and he avoided intimacy to avoid the emotional cost of loss. Sex therapists are often presented with situations in which men report a good history of sexual functioning until they experience a "relationship-deepening event." Recall that relationship-deepening events can be any significant indicator that the relationship is becoming more serious, and the risk of emotional vulnerability has intensified. Such events may be moving in with a partner, getting engaged/married/committed, the birth of a child, etc. The list goes on and on depending upon what circumstance threatens the existence of the man and triggers the sexual shutdown. Suzanne Iasenza (2020) opines that sex is usually good at the start of a relationship, but when partners become more familiar with and committed to each other, relational narratives kick in unconsciously (p. 9). She often tells her clients: When it comes to sex, our minds are not our friends (p. 11). While I certainly understand her point and the fact that our unconscious minds or narratives can create substantial problems, particularly sexual problems, I would suggest that when it comes to sex, our mind does try to be our friend. Once the trauma is triggered in the unconscious mind, Yalom's "protective process" kicks in. This protective process creates a sexual impediment or shutdown in an effort to protect us from further injury or reinjury. In existential sex therapy, we are looking at the penis as the communicator of male fears of vulnerability, exposure, and emotional nakedness. In other words, the penis reacts to perceived threats to one's existence. When attempting to unravel the meaning behind the penis's protective shutdown, we look particularly for the existential themes described by Yalom (1980), i.e., isolation, freedom and responsibility, lack of meaning, and death. Let's examine some case examples to see how these psychological leitmotifs play out.

Existential Sex Therapy in Practice

The practice of sex therapy and psychotherapy can be done utilizing many different modes and theoretical orientations. Yalom reminds us that existential psychotherapy does not represent a standard set of techniques, styles, or protocols. The concepts of existential therapy can be best understood as a lens or guide by which psychotherapy is practiced. Practitioners of all theoretical philosophies can bring an existential perspective to their treatment process.

When I treat my male sex therapy patients, I follow a similar pattern with all as a starting point. Whether I am treating an individual male or a couple, I like to begin by asking about what brings them in to see me and allow the story to unfold in whatever manner they choose. I am particularly interested in the description of the problem, the conditions under which the problem manifests itself, and the timeline regarding when the symptom first presented. My goal is to begin to get an understanding of the meaning and protective/adaptive purpose the sexual difficulty may represent. Typically, men will present with little to no insight as to the reason for their sexual shutdown. They often describe a generally satisfying relationship with a partner they find attractive. Most of the men I treat, especially those experiencing erectile difficulties, will report relative ease at attaining penile tumescence, and engorgement will be maintained through extended periods of sexual foreplay. But the erection fades as intercourse approaches or shortly after penetration occurs. Typically, these men reveal a current history of satisfying and frequent masturbation. They will often express a vague notion of being anxious about sexual function and a firm belief that their penile difficulties have some medical basis. However, they are at a loss to explain how a physical or medical issue allows for erections that are fully functional during masturbation but not penetrative sex. Their partners are similarly stymied.

Following the initial consultation, I will focus on family and developmental history. If I'm treating a couple, I will ask to do three individual sessions with each before resuming couples' work. It is important to me to develop a good understanding of each person's experience in his or her family of origin and to identify any patterns of trauma that might be getting triggered in the current relationship. I want to learn about the personalities of family members, their relationship with each of them, and their relationship with each other. I want to know if this was a family that was able to communicate about and/or demonstrate emotions or if theirs was a family of secrets and repressed suffering. I want to know if there was any presence of substance abuse or domestic violence and/or parental neglect/over-involvement. In essence, I am looking to gain an appreciation for any family dynamic that may have felt threatening that could be reenacting itself in the current relationship and, thereby, creating a threat to the man's existence and well-being.

Many highly regarded sex therapists will spend a great deal of time taking an in-depth sexual history. I do not, as I find much of the information in a standard sex history to be irrelevant, particularly in those men who have had a prior history of good sexual functioning. Through an existential lens, the sexual "problem" is often not about how the man feels about sex per se. The problem is more typically understood as an attempt for the man's penis to communicate some deep anxiety, concern, and existential threat to his existence. Therefore, to more fully comprehend the message the penis is sending, a comprehensive developmental/family-of-origin/relational history will be of greater value. Let's consider the case of Russ from the perspective of an existentially oriented sex therapist.

The Case of Russ

Fifty-one-year-old Russ came to see me shortly after his wedding to Sarah. This was a first marriage for Russ and the second for Sarah. Both had come from traumatic families of origin, and Sarah's first marriage was to a man who regularly abused her. Russ's primary complaint was a lifelong inability to ejaculate. I began by asking Russ for a timeline regarding his ejaculatory difficulties. I have found that the time of onset of problematic sexual symptoms is often of great significance in understanding what may be triggering the current inhibition. While most men presenting with this complaint have their ejaculatory difficulty limited to their time with a partner and have little to no difficulty ejaculating during masturbation, Russ reported that Sarah was his first sexual partner, and ejaculation during masturbation was problematic as well, although it would occur on occasion. Given the unusualness of this situation, I asked if Russ had consulted a urologist or other physician, and he indicated that it was his urologist who provided him the referral to me. His urologist did not detect any medical explanation for Russ's ejaculation problem.

We next began to talk about Russ's upbringing and family of origin. Russ came from a family with two professionally educated parents, both of whom enjoyed great professional success and respect. They also were rather puritanical and punitive. Russ was the oldest of four children, and the siblings all have minimal interaction with each other. Despite the fine professional reputation his parents possessed, Russ recalls them as constantly fighting, explosively angry, sleeping in separate rooms, engaging in multiple infidelities, and hardly being civil to each other. Neither had much to do with the children, his father due to excessive alcohol use and his mother using her work to avoid being at home. He recalls his mother telling him in a fit of rage that she never wanted to be a mother and blamed his father for forcing parenthood on her.

Russ also reported that laughter, enjoyment, and pleasure were not only absent in his home but were considered sinful and to be averted at all costs. Any expressions of joy were severely reprimanded and punished. As a result, Russ learned as a young boy to repress any feelings or demonstrations of delight, joyfulness, and pleasure. He recalled that to the present day, if he is enjoying a television show or a musical piece, he will turn it off. He does not enjoy comedians or most other forms of entertainment. His free time is spent reading serious, nonfiction books and tinkering with electronic devices. Regarding the specifics of sex, he reports a strong libido and easy arousal, but he begins to panic as he approaches ejaculation and, thus, ceases all stimulation. In addition to shutting down all sensations of pleasure, Russ reports learning to be exquisitely attuned to the displeasure of his parents. He was constantly scanning the home environment to head off any actions or commotions that would rouse the ire of his chronically unhappy and volatile parents.

Russ grew up a very lonely child. Despite having three siblings, the home was minimally interactive, and Russ did all he could to avoid other family members. He spent a great deal of time alone in his bedroom or in the local branch library. He recalls few friendships with schoolmates, as his parents discouraged such contacts. His activities were primarily solo, and this pattern continued through college and his career. In high school, Russ discovered a love of the sciences, and he decided to pursue a career in medicine. While he enjoyed his studies, he found his clinical rotations to be laborious. For a time, Russ thought he had made a poor career choice until he discovered the field of pathology. Pathology afforded him the solitude he found comforting as well as the opportunity to pursue his interest in lab sciences. In addition, being a pathologist required minimal interaction with colleagues, offered steady, predictable hours, and relieved Russ of the burden of having to deal directly with patients. He had a reputation at work as a hardworking and dependable physician but also as a loner who showed little interest in the lives of his co-workers. Oddly, his workplace was where he met the person who would dramatically alter his life's course, Sarah.

Sarah was a pathologist in the same lab as Russ. She was also a serious-minded and reserved person, but she was more social and outgoing than was Russ. She found Russ to be appealing for several reasons. She liked that he was smart, hardworking, and seemingly uninterested in office gossip and politics. She also discovered Russ's dry, witty sense of humor as being particularly self-effacing and clever. She decided to ask him to join her for dinner one evening, and Russ, to his surprise, accepted.

Russ did not date and reports no prior relationships before meeting Sarah. He was quite taken aback when Sarah invited him to dinner, as no other women had ever pursued him. He liked Sarah, thought she was beautiful, and found her laugh to be quite charming. She always seemed to genuinely enjoy her conversations with him, and this was a most unfamiliar experience. Russ recalls being nervous before the date but also excited to go. He reported they had a surprisingly nice evening, and he felt a lightness that was both strange and pleasing. He very much

wanted to continue dating Sarah. Fortunately, Sarah, too, recalled enjoying her evening with Russ, and the two began to spend a considerable
amount of nonworking time together. Sex proceeded slowly, which was
fine for them both. Russ was unable to ejaculate during intercourse and
soon began to develop erectile difficulties. Russ found erections fairly
easy to achieve and maintain until it was time for vaginal penetration.
Russ would then begin to lose tumescence. Sarah was unflustered and
patient, but Russ was frustrated. He wanted to be able to fully experience
sex with Sarah, mostly because he did not want her to feel bad or worry
that he wasn't attracted to/interested in her.

It seemed readily apparent to me that Russ's traumatic upbringing was
affecting his sexual functioning. His penis was speaking to him and cau-
tioning him against allowing himself to be vulnerable to others. We spent
a good deal of time discussing his family of origin and how his penis
might be trying to send him a message of prudence. Existentially, Russ
suffered from fears of mortality and isolation. Specifically, Russ found
his existence threatened by his feelings of vulnerability with Sarah. His
past relationships with family left him vigilant against allowing others
to get close and potentially harm him. He had spent most of his life as a
loner, and this allowed him to feel protected and safe. However, meeting Sarah made him aware of the depth of his loneliness, and he longed
for companionship and love. While his conscious mind was telling him
how wonderful life with Sarah would be, his protective unconscious was
alerting him to the peril and fragility of his existence should he allow
himself to be exposed and laid bare to another. The threat of hurt, rejection, and grief was palpable as Russ continued to deepen his affection
and connection to Sarah.

In addition to the threat of annihilation, Russ also was becoming
increasingly aware of his isolation from self. His perpetual scanning of
his childhood home environment and vigilance for any signs of upset
from his parents made him unaware of what his own needs were. That,
combined with the family's disdain for anything pleasurable, left Russ
in a constant state of anxiety during partnered sex. When in sexual situations with Sarah, Russ was so preoccupied with whether Sarah was
responding positively that he was oblivious to his own sense of sexual
arousal. Psychotherapy focused on Russ allowing himself to become
comfortable with experiencing nonsexual pleasure and then moving

to sexual pleasure during solo masturbation. A combination of dealing with the trauma of his childhood environment along with some directed behavioral suggestions allowed this to be accomplished over a period of several months.

Allowing himself to ejaculate during his time with Sarah proved more challenging, and improvements came about in small, inconsistent increments. Russ's ability to fully let go when in the presence of another was (not surprisingly) difficult to overcome. Russ's childhood home taught him to self-protectively be on guard against the ire of his warring parents. Hypervigilance in the presence of others became his lifelong strategy for survival. Overcoming the trauma of his childhood took considerable work in psychotherapy, but eventually, Russ was able to ejaculate in Sarah's presence. First, he was able to ejaculate in her presence via solo masturbation. This then progressed to Sarah being able to bring Russ to ejaculation using her hand, and eventually, Russ was able to ejaculate during sexual intercourse. Each of these successive advances occurred inconsistently for quite some time but gradually became easier and easier to achieve. During times of emotional stress/dysregulation on either of their parts, Russ will regress, but such regressions are temporary and typically resolve in a matter of days to weeks. Both Russ and Sarah are pleased with their movement, and treatment is ongoing.

Russ and Sarah's story illustrates many of the seminal points in existential sex therapy. Note the existential concerns of a threatened existence and the penis speaking through a self-protective shutdown of sexual functioning. Russ feared his existence would be snuffed out if he allowed himself to be emotionally close to Sarah or allow himself to feel joy/pleasure. In addition, Russ became increasingly aware of his isolation from himself. When with Sarah, he was so consumed with scanning her reactions that he completely lost sight of his own desires. Russ's anxiety about displeasing another meant that the only time he felt sexually comfortable was during solo sexual activity, when he could focus exclusively on himself with no distraction.

Russ was a man who was deeply untrusting of others, and this, along with his isolation from self, negatively affected his budding relationship with Sarah. While what makes psychotherapy work is always somewhat mysterious, it seems clear to me that a significant aspect of

Russ's improvement was the quality of the therapeutic relationship built between the two of us. Over time, Russ came to trust that my interest in him and his well-being was genuine. As his comfort with me increased, Russ was able to take more risks in therapy and reveal more and more of himself. In addition, he was able to venture into unexplored territory as he began to learn more about himself, his feelings, his fears, and his desires. Existential sex therapy, like existential psychotherapy, is rooted in the depth of the therapeutic relationship. The elements of connection, genuineness, compassion, and safety are the most potent tools available to the practicing sex therapist.

I am often asked if behavioral sex therapy exercises have a place in existential sex therapy. While I tend to use them sparingly, they certainly have an important place in providing some immediate relief of symptoms and encouraging patients to take risks and move forward. However, I believe that a therapy that was primarily based in behavioral exercises would have been ultimately ineffective for Russ. Russ had suffered so much damage from his family of origin that without doing deep trauma work with an existential lens, he would not have allowed himself to move toward tolerating the experience of pleasure. In addition, exercises that focused directly on the functioning of his penis would have been of little value until Russ better understood the messages of anxiety and trauma being communicated to him through his penis. Frankl's process of dereflection allowed Russ to focus on triggering of childhood trauma and allow his protective unconscious to loosen its grip. Still, behavioral suggestions clearly had a place in Russ's treatment, as merely working through the trauma of childhood would not have given him the sexual skills he required. I am often reminded of one of Yalom's (1980, 2002a) most important axioms: "Insight without action is merely interesting." All good therapy needs to move the patient beyond the point of insight to take the necessary emotional risks to make use of such insights and awarenesses. As a result, even though the bulk of my therapy focuses on deep reflection and insight to assist the man in better understanding the message his penis is sending him, I often find behavioral exercises or suggestions to be of great value.

Let's examine another case that illustrates the principles and process of existential sex therapy.

The Case of Ascher

Ascher was a 44-year-old man who had been married for 21 years to Marcie. Both reported a generally satisfying relationship that had recently become distressed due to Marcie's discovery of Asher's many infidelities. Ascher admitted to frequent use of pornography, chatrooms, and sex workers. Marcie discovered Ascher's transgressions after being diagnosed with a sexually transmitted infection at a routine GYN exam.

Both Ascher and Marcie were religiously observant, and sexual intercourse was not attempted until after marriage. Sex seemed to proceed smoothly with little complication for the first 12 to 24 months of marriage. Both reported a high level of sexual satisfaction during this time. However, Ascher began to pull away from Marcie sexually, and their sexual frequency quickly diminished. When Marcie questioned Ascher about his apparent sexual avoidance, he offered some vague explanations and vowed to increase the frequency of his sexual initiations. Ascher did begin to initiate sex more often, but then he often would experience erectile loss just prior to vaginal penetration. Both Ascher and Marcie found this distressing, but Ascher was reluctant to consult his physician and instead just drifted further away from Marcie sexually. Marcie was troubled by Ascher's lack of interest in pursuing an answer to this conundrum, and the two began to fight repeatedly. It was later discovered that Ascher's reluctance to consult his physician was due to his awareness that his erectile difficulties did not occur during solo masturbation or interactions with sex workers. Had Marcie not been diagnosed with an STI, this cycle of sexual avoidance may have continued indefinitely, as divorce was not a consideration for either of them.

Ascher agreed to begin psychotherapy and consulted a "sex addiction specialist." Sex addiction therapy proceeded for about a year, but improvement was minimal. Therapy focused primarily on behavioral interventions designed to control Ascher's urges to sexually "act out," as well as regular attendance at a 12-step sex addiction group. Ascher reported enjoying both the individual therapy and the group meetings and found the support he received from both to be very meaningful. However, Ascher felt that his issues were not being adequately identified and addressed, and change was negligible. Both Ascher and Marcie were frustrated by the lack of progress, and they were referred to me for an alternative approach to the problem.

My initial meeting was with both Ascher and Marcie, but their wish was for Ascher to receive individual psychotherapy. Marcie attended the session to be supportive and offer to be helpful in any way she was needed. However, Ascher felt he needed to "confront his inner demons" and wanted to do this via individual treatment. I agreed, as I thought Ascher's difficulties preceded and were separate from his relationship with Marcie, and we agreed to begin individual therapy with the idea of bringing Marcie into the therapy at a later point if necessary.

Ascher and I began by discussing the onset of his problematic behavior. He reported that he had never felt sexually conflicted or compulsive prior to his marriage to Marcie. He reported loving Marcie and thought she was an outstanding wife, mother, and friend. He found his behavior puzzling, as he found her sexually attractive and enjoyed sex with her greatly. We also discussed his prior psychotherapy and what he found helpful and not helpful about it. Ascher recalled liking his therapist and felt great relief at being able to discuss what he had been keeping hidden for so long. He also enjoyed the support and camaraderie of the 12-step group but had a nagging sense that as inconceivable as it was to him, his problem was not really about sex, which was the sole focus of his prior therapy and the 12-step group. I asked him if his problem was not about sex, what did he think it was about, but he had no answer and found his situation to be quite puzzling.

We next began to talk about Ascher's family of origin and childhood memories. Ascher was the oldest of five boys born to a religiously observant mother and father. He reports a generally happy home environment in which the laws and rituals of Judaism were practiced, celebrated, and enforced. Ascher was educated in Jewish day schools, where he received both secular and nonsecular education. He recalls enjoying school and being a very good and popular student. Ascher was very much committed to his religious teachings and practices but recollects always fighting a desire to rebel. He didn't mind or object to any of his religious obligations but always felt an objection to being "controlled." Ascher described himself as being an intensely curious youngster who frequently questioned the absoluteness of rabbinic authority and wanted to know what the "forbidden" experiences would be like. He had questions about the laws of kashrut (the requirement to keep a kosher diet) and often felt a strong urge to sample nonkosher food and, on occasion, did secretly indulge. As an adolescent, Ascher experienced the expected sexual urges and desires and would occasionally allow himself to masturbate. These transgressions left him feeling guilty but pleased by his displays of autonomy and independence. Again, it was not that Ascher felt forced into a life of religious observance that he did not want, but Ascher abjured feeling controlled, stifled, and limited.

Ascher reported that while he was eager to marry Marcie, he felt rather quickly like marriage was "suffocating." This feeling was quite surprising to him, since he believed he enjoyed being with Marcie a great deal. Nevertheless, marriage quickly felt confining, limiting, and controlling. Since Ascher did not engage in premarital sex, he did not know how he would have behaved sexually in another relationship with someone besides Marcie, but he suspects he may have felt suffocated in any relationship that removed his ability to feel as if he had choices.

It was becoming increasingly clear that Ascher was reacting to feelings of being controlled (losing his autonomy) and suffocated. Existentially, this would correspond to Yalom's (1980) dilemmas of freedom and mortality. Ascher's problematic sexual behavior was likely his response to these internal and unacknowledged conflicts, much like his desire to sneak nonkosher foods when a young boy.

When I mentioned this to Ascher, he responded immediately and enthusiastically that this conceptualization resonated strongly. Ascher then described the strong obligation he felt to not disappoint his parents or to be poor role model for his brothers. Throughout his life, he felt both proud of and burdened with these responsibilities. The combination of family and religious obligation often made Ascher feel as if his life was not his own, and he struggled with his desires for freedom and autonomy against the perceived constraints imbedded in so much of his life. He reported never having expressed these feelings to anyone before, and this was never explored in his prior therapy. As our discussion continued over the weeks and months, it became increasingly clear to Ascher why he was behaving as he was, and he felt that now that he had a substantially greater insight into the meaning behind his actions, he would have an easier time dealing with them. It was now time to ask Marcie to rejoin the therapy.

Marcie was pleased to participate in the therapy, and she had been doing important work on herself in individual therapy. She reported being pleased with Ascher's new understandings and insights but found herself struggling with issues of trust. Her existence now also felt threatened, as she saw Ascher as not only someone she loved but also as someone who had the ability to do her great harm and destroy the life that she loved. It was determined that they would be best served by another psychotherapist for couples' therapy, since Ascher wished to continue his individual therapy and growth with me. Both Ascher and Marcie agreed that this was the best way to go, and I referred them to one of my colleagues who did couples' work. At the time of this writing, Ascher continues a productive individual psychotherapy with me, and the two of them are doing well in couples' therapy, having recently begun resuming their sexual relationship.

The case of Ascher again highlights how the penis speaks for distressed men. Ascher shut down sexually when he began feeling suffocated and constrained. First, he pulled away sexually from Marcie. This was of great concern for her, and she began to push Ascher for an explanation. Since Ascher felt unable to express his feelings for fear of acknowledging his "less than pure" urges, he subordinated his emotions and tried to bypass them. He then tried to accede to Marcie's wishes and continue to interact sexually with her, but his protective unconscious would not let his penis function, and the sexual shutdown took a much-harder-to-explain path. All of this was further complicated by Ascher's frequent use of pornography and sex workers. These outlets, while making Ascher feel extremely guilty, also provided him with the "reassurance" that he was not being controlled and still possessed the autonomy to rebel against expectations. Given the internal conflicts Ascher was battling, it is little wonder that a therapy primarily focused on behavioral exercises designed to increase sexual interest and improve erectile functioning fell short. Ascher's protective unconscious would thwart all efforts to move into territory that created an existential threat to him. Until those unacknowledged and unexpressed conflicts had been exposed, Ascher was unable to understand, and therefore change, any of his problematic behaviors.

Oftentimes, behavioral sex therapy's treatment failures alert us to the possibility that something else is going on, and it is in these cases that an exploration of existential issues may be most helpful. In the case of Ascher and Marcie, we see that once again, the penis speaks and, according to well-known psychologist and sex therapist Kathryn S.K. Hall, sometimes it yells (personal communication, 12/03/2021)!

In this chapter, we have explored many of the most salient features of existential sex therapy and how sex therapy with an existential lens differs from most traditional forms of sex therapy. Ascher's case provides us with an excellent transition to our next chapter, hypersexuality, or what is often referred to as sex addiction. Many of the patients we see in sex therapy practice are not suffering from a sexual shutdown but what appears to be quite the opposite—a pattern of sexual behavior that they find difficult to control and manage. The existential issues in cases of hypersexuality are often most closely aligned with fears of death and mortality. Let's take the next step in understanding this complicated and difficult-to-treat phenomenon and the messages the penis is sending.

5

HYPERSEXUALITY, SEX ADDICTION, OUT-OF-CONTROL SEXUAL BEHAVIOR

A Diagnostic Dilemma?

One of the more hotly debated topics in sex therapy today is the theoretical and clinical construct commonly referred to as "sexual addiction." Clinicians and researchers have been deliberating for years how to describe, categorize, diagnose, and treat the phenomenon of sexual behavior that appears to be uncontrollable, irrepressible, and compulsive. Many have argued that this behavioral pattern is consistent with behavior we have typically termed addictive (Carnes, 1994, 2001; Schaumburg, 1997), while others have vehemently disputed this conceptualization and suggest that an addiction model of interpreting and treating this clinical presentation is ill informed and ineffectual (Moser, 2011; Ley, 2014; Braun-Harvey & Vigorito, 2015). The lack of agreement and specificity regarding the assessment and diagnostic criteria has led Grubbs et al. (2017) to comment that such debate clouds the reality that many people continue to suffer with sexual behavior they find difficult to control. This results in the human elements of suffering being buried in a futile intellectual wrangle.

Fortunately, for the existential therapist, this is a dispute that has little meaning or importance. Recall that the existential therapist is not

DOI: 10.4324/9781003127871-6

concerned with diagnostic labels, as they are considered limiting and reductionistic. Rather, for the existential therapist, each person sitting in front of us has his or her own story and unique set of circumstances that define their pattern of problematic behavior. As mentioned earlier in this book, existential therapy strives to recognize the uniqueness of each individual and create a new and different therapy for each person. While not an existential therapist himself, the perspective of the existential therapist may be best summed up by Toronto-based psychologist James Cantor and colleagues (Cantor et al., 2013) when they assert:

> Despite that the literature emphasizes that cases of hypersexuality are highly diverse with regard to clinical presentation and comorbid features, the major models for understanding and treating hypersexuality employ a "one-size-fits-all" approach. That is, rather than identify which problematic behaviors might respond best to which interventions, existing approaches presume or assert without evidence that all cases of hypersexuality (however termed or defined) represent the same underlying problem and merit the same approach to intervention.
>
> (p. 883)

Cantor et al. recognize that the same pattern of behavior may occur for many different reasons in different men. This is consistent with the existential therapy perspective that strives to create a new therapy for each person to recognize the individuality of the man and the meaning the behavior might have for him.

Most of the patients that I see complaining of lack of control over their sexual behavior come to therapy using the popular term "sex addiction." As a result, I will often use this term when discussing their sexual issues even though I do not practice from an addiction model of treatment. Many of my male patients have had experiences like those of Ascher, whose story was examined in the previous chapter. Ascher had initially received treatment based on a sex-addiction model (individual therapy combined with a 12-step sex addiction group), an approach that is quite popular in the United States today. While Ascher did report benefits from the treatment, his sexual behavior remained unchanged. Often, when such treatments are ineffective, it is because there are some deeply hidden underlying issues that have remained unaddressed. Existential sex therapy looks to identify and attend to the unacknowledged and therefore unresolved existential dilemmas that are haunting these men.

Several years ago, I noticed a frequently occurring pattern in many of the men I treated for uncontrollable sexual behavior. When asking about family-of-origin issues, I discovered that many of these men had experienced early childhood losses, most typically the death of a father or other caretaker. This phenomenon was introduced earlier in Chapter 3. There, we examined the impact early death of a father had on many men's lives in a general sense, but in this chapter, we will explore more specifically the sway that such traumatic events have over men's sexual behavior. By now, I have collected dozens of case studies of men whose uncontrolled (and uncharacteristic) sexual behavior was preceded by a confrontation with mortality. Interestingly, many of these experiences occurred as these men approached the age of their young, deceased fathers. Note the use of the term "uncharacteristic." Most of the men that I have treated for these conditions report never having sexual behavior control issues before their confrontation with life's impermanence. As with all cases of psychotherapy, I am of the firm belief that the timing of when the problematic behavior began is of great importance in understanding the meaning and protective function of the presenting symptom. It is unfortunate that this perspective is not more widespread among clinicians, especially when treating sexual control issues. Typical therapy protocols for these issues focus on controlling rather than understanding the oftentimes cryptic messages being sent from the protective unconscious to the penis.

In addition to being uncharacteristic, much of these men's problematic uncontrolled sexual behavior represents a behavioral escalation and increased level of risk, peril, and danger. Ford and colleagues (2004) conducted a study of college undergraduates who were asked to complete questionnaires assessing their sexual activity of the prior week. They then received a lecture on mortality and were dismissed from class for the weekend. At the next class, they were again asked to complete the same measures of sexual activity, this time for the week following the lecture on mortality, and the results were remarkably noteworthy. Following the lecture on mortality, students reported a significant increase in sexual frequency and risky sexual behavior (i.e., random hook-ups, unprotected sex, sex in more conspicuous places, etc.). In other words, what Ford et al. were able to demonstrate was not only that sexual behavior increased following the introduction of the salience of mortality but that it also increased in ways that were uncharacteristic of the students' typical sexual behavior patterns. Simply being reminded of the closeness of death to us all caused great discomfort among Ford's students. You may recall from Chapter 3 my experience when giving a talk about sex and death to the Society of Sex Therapy and Research, I received only a modest amount of applause. However, the next day, several of my colleagues reported to me that they had slept fitfully the evening before! While we may not be consciously aware, there is often prodigious disquiet when we are confronted with the awareness that death is inescapable.

As mentioned earlier, the pandemic has seen an increase in sexual fantasies, pornography consumption, and solitary sexual activity (Cascalheira et al., 2021). While this may seem to be a benign finding, as we explore the relationship between death terror and sexual behavior, it raises the strong possibility that the significance of these sexual increases is much more profound than we may initially realize. In addition, we again see sexual behavior becoming uncharacteristically intensified in the face of death terror and death anxiety resulting from the horrors of the COVID-19 contagion.

Yalom (2002b, 2015) has repeatedly stated that concerns about death often manifest in the preoccupation with sexual thoughts and behaviors. Sex is often experienced as a life force, the antithesis of death. As a result, sex is regularly utilized as a means of neutralizing the terror of the realization that one's existence will end. Yalom (1980) has also observed that many of his patients diagnosed with a life-threatening illness will uncharacteristically increase their sexual interests and activities in an attempt to repress their sense of overpowering anxiety. In his 2008 text *Staring at the Sun: Overcoming the Terror of Death*, Yalom writes:

> *Sex, the vital life force, often counters thoughts of death. I've encountered many instances of this mechanism: the patient with a severe coronary who was so sexually driven that in an ambulance carrying him to the emergency room, he attempted to grope an ambulance attendant; or the widow who felt overcome with sexual feelings while driving to her husband's funeral; or the elderly widower, terrified by death, who became uncharacteristically sexually driven and had so many sexual affairs with women in his retirement community and created such divisiveness that the management demanded he seek psychiatric consultation. Still another elderly woman, after her twin sister had died from a stroke, became so overcome with multiple orgasms while using a vibrator that she feared she too would suffer a stroke.*

(pp. 212–213)

Similarly, Yalom (1980) recalls the words of University of Washington professor of nursing Patricia MacElveen-Hoehn describing some of her clinical observations:

> the sexually conservative woman who returns home for the funeral of a parent or some close relative and takes with her a diaphragm and uncharacteristically engages in a sexual relationship with a stranger or casual friend; or the man who has a severe coronary and on the way to the hospital fondles his wife's breasts and presses for some sexual exchange; or the man who, with a child dying of leukemia, becomes highly promiscuous.
>
> (p. 145)

It is noteworthy that both Yalom and MacElveen-Hoehn describe the behavior of these patients as *uncharacteristic*. None of them reported concerns with sexual behavior prior to the triggering of their terror of death precipitated by a confrontation with mortality. In the face of death and a stark reminder of their own mortality, their sexual behavior presented in an insistent and irrepressible manner in an apparent struggle to ward off the fear and dread of extinction.

It seems apropos to reiterate that as mentioned in Chapter 3, Yalom, too, finds that sexual thoughts invade his awareness in the face of the death of his beloved wife, Marilyn, and the ever-creeping awareness that his own mortality and existence is palpable. He notes in the book he and his wife, Marilyn, co-wrote as they were facing her imminent death from cancer (2021):

> But now, a new obsession has invaded my thoughts: whenever I relax and try to clear my mind, for instance awaiting sleep after turning out the lights, I am visited by enticing sexual thoughts involving women I've known or seen recently. These images are powerful and persistent. I try to block them, purge them from consciousness, turn my thoughts elsewhere. But, a few minutes later, they reappear and again seize my attention. I am flooded with both desire and shame. I wince at such disloyalty to Marilyn, buried only a few weeks ago.
>
> As I look back over the last few weeks, I've also become aware of a curious (and embarrassing) development: intensified interest in women's breasts, especially sizable breasts . . .
>
> I am unsettled and ashamed of these sexual obsessions. A debate proceeds in my mind. How could I so dishonor myself and my love

for Marilyn? Is this really how shallow my love is? But, on the other hand, isn't it my task now to stay alive, to begin a new life?

(pp. 169–170)

Note some of the words that Yalom uses to describe his emotional state. He references feeling an obsession, persistent, intensified, and alive. Certainly, many of these thoughts and emotions are typical of men who are grieving and experiencing concerns related to their own mortality, and while there is no indication that Yalom was unable to resist his feelings exploding, he does report many of the sentiments of those cases in which a man's sexual behavior has become highly problematic.

Let us now examine a sampling of the cases of I have seen of men who describe their sexual behavior as feeling compulsive, insistent, uncharacteristically amplified, and uncontrollable. But first, let me voice a case seen by Yalom (1980):

> Tim was a 30-year-old patient whose wife was dying of leukemia. Tim began therapy not because of overt grief but because of an alarming degree of sexual preoccupation and compulsivity. He had led a monogamous life prior to his wife's illness, but as she approached death, he began compulsively to visit pornography films and singles' bars (running great risks of public exposure) and masturbated several times a day, often while in bed with his dying wife. On the night of his wife's funeral, he sought out a prostitute.
>
> (p. 145)

Tim's case illustrates many of the dynamics we've been examining, particularly the uncharacteristic explosion of sexual behavior and the optics of great insensitivity toward a partner. What makes Tim's case noteworthy, though, is the youthful age of him and his wife. Not only was Tim likely experiencing tremendous grief but also colossal fear. If death could visit his young wife, why could death not come for him as well? While I have no doubt that Tim's grief was profound, it is likely that his ravenous pursuit of sex was an attempt to ward off the unconscious and unacknowledged terror of his own demise.

I have now seen dozens of men whose sexual behavior became unmanageable following a confrontation with mortality. Most were unable to identify a link between his problematic sexual behavior and death terror until sex therapy progressed. Each of the following men self-identified as sex addicts with no awareness of what was driving their behavior other than some type of "addiction" or "disease." However, a thorough exploration of family-of-origin and developmental history was able to uncover a death anxiety provocation that was proximate to their uncharacteristic and turbulent sexual changes.

The Case of Donald

Donald was a 54-year-old married man who sought consultation for "sexual addiction." He reported a 25-year stable, monogamous, and "vanilla," marriage as well as a high degree of satisfaction with his work, family, and sexual life. Donald's family of origin was notable for the untimely and unexpected death of his father at age 53. Donald's father suffered a heart attack that deeply affected Donald and his family. The death of his father was particularly frightening for Donald since it occurred while he and his father were fishing in a rowboat at a nearby lake. The day appeared like many others except for Donald's father complaining of some nonspecific stomach pain. About two hours after leaving shore, Donald's father slumped over, and young Donald panicked, not knowing what to do. Eventually, Donald rowed to shore and screamed for help, but by that time, his father was already lifeless. Donald was overcome with grief and guilt for not being able to help his father, and he reported feeling intermittently depressed and melancholy since. The ghost of Donald's father haunted him on a regular basis. Much like the experiences described in Louden Wainright III's album *Older Than My Old Man Now* (see Chapter 3), and particularly since his 50th birthday, Donald felt his father's staunch presence and lived with the nagging sense that he, too, would die an early death and not live beyond the age of his deceased father.

As Donald approached his 54th birthday, he recalled a profound sense of relief that he would live beyond the age of his father. However, one week before Donald's 54th birthday, his doctor called to inform him of a dramatically elevated PSA and the need for an immediate prostate biopsy. Donald felt a cloud of doom form over him, and this was intensified by his physician's diagnosis of prostate cancer and recommendation of a radical prostatectomy. Despite his physician's reassurance that they discovered his prostate cancer early and his prospects for recovery were excellent, Donald could not shake the sense of foreboding that now engulfed him, and he began to experience panic attacks.

Approximately 6 months after his radical prostatectomy, Donald began to patronize massage parlors, strip clubs, and sex workers suddenly and uncharacteristically. Donald reported his behavior feeling "compulsive," "insistent," "obsessive," and "uncontrollable." As time passed, his atypical sexual behavior escalated in frequency, range, and risk, and he impulsively quit his job, left his wife and children, and began a feverish journey around the country, seeking solace through sexual conquest and adventure. He had sexual interactions with both women and men (for the first time), and although he was unable to identify what was driving his current level of interest and activity, he felt unable to cease the chase or find peace in his sexual escapades. After repeated sexual frustrations due to his inability to achieve penile erection (a consequence of his radical prostatectomy), Donald procured a hotel room in Chicago, Illinois, and attempted suicide by an overdose of prescribed medication. Fortunately, Donald's suicide attempt resulted in only a prolonged sleep, and upon awakening, he called for help. After a brief hospitalization, Donald returned home and sought psychotherapy.

Psychotherapy began with an exploration of Donald's current situation, and then I proceeded to learn the story of Donald's life and development. It was there that the link was made between the tragic and traumatic death of Donald's father and the timing of his sexual changes. Indeed, Donald's recollection of seeking his first same-sex experiences was an attempt to feel "alive" and to seek a "spark" to life. We then explored Donald's longstanding fears of his own mortality and the vulnerability he lived with for much of his life. Just this change in narrative was of great benefit to Donald in that he was able to see that his difficulties did not lie in some outside entity such as a disease state of an addiction but rather were the product of the inner triggering of early childhood trauma that he could have some influence and control over. Donald's sense of hopelessness began to fade, and he returned to his family, friends, and job. Much of our therapy dealt with the grief, loss, and existential uncertainties that often accompany early life trauma. Donald reported feeling greatly settled by the therapeutic exploration and the psychotherapy process. In Donald's life, this period was an aberration, and Donald reported being able to return to a life that was fulfilling, satisfying, and meaningful to him.

Donald's case, while somewhat extreme in its presentation, is very typical of the existential issues and crises that can lead to uncharacteristic and problematic sexual behavior. Keep in mind that prior to his cancer diagnosis and direct confrontation with his own mortality, Donald's sexual life was what he described as "vanilla." Also notable here is that Donald's precipitous sentience regarding his own demise triggered his repressed death terror that resulted from his early traumatic loss. Had Donald not experienced the trauma of early loss, he very likely would have been able to manage his anxiety about his cancer in a less chaotic and problematic manner. Recall that one of the basic tenets of existential sex therapy is that an event occurs that triggers early trauma. This sets off an unconscious self-protective spiral in which the penis becomes the conduit for the message of danger and a warning sign of a perceived threat to one's existence.

Let's examine another case of problematic sexual behavior being triggered by an existential death-terror crisis.

The Case of Nicholas

Nicholas was a 49- year-old male who was facing his third unwanted divorce. Each of his divorces was precipitated by his wives' discovery of his many infidelities. His most recent sexual transgression was with his current wife's first cousin. Nicholas presented for therapy in a state of great distress and confusion. He was completely dumbfounded by his recurring behavior, as he reported being happily married to each of his wives and having enjoyed sex with all of them. He reported that each of his wives knew only a fraction of his extramarital escapades, and he estimated having sex with well over one hundred women during his marriages. Nicholas described his behavior as unwanted, intrusive, compulsive, and irrepressible. Despite avowing a strong desire to stop his problematic sexual behavior, he found himself unable to cease pursuing women.

Nicholas recalled a difficult childhood. His mother suffered from severe mental illness and was often hospitalized for lengthy periods following multiple suicide attempts. Her illness was so profound that even when at home, she was unable to care for Nicholas and his two younger siblings. Tragically, Nicholas's father died young from a massive heart attack, and young Nicholas was left to provide much of the childcare, home management, and care for his mother. Of course, this was quite burdensome for Nicholas, who was still under 12 years old. Nevertheless, he did what needed to be done and sacrificed much of his childhood to care for his family.

While Nicholas's story was filled with tragic circumstances, I was most drawn to the early death of his father as a likely precipitant for his sexual behavior. I asked Nicholas if he could recall when his sexual behavior became unmanageable. He replied quickly that he was very clear on the timing of when sex changed for him. He said it was just after his 35th birthday. I then asked Nicholas at what age his father died, fully expecting to hear that he died at age 35, but Nicholas responded that his father died at age 62. My surprise at not receiving the answer I was expecting must have been more obvious than I realized, as Nicholas asked me if something was wrong. I said of course not and explained to him that I had seen many men who were experiencing problematic sexual behavior upon reaching the age at which their young fathers died, and he reiterated that was not the case for his dad.

We then continued our conversation about background and family of origin until suddenly, Nicholas stopped speaking and appeared almost frozen. I inquired as to what just happened, and he replied, "Holy shit. I just remembered that while it is accurate that my father died at 62 from a massive heart attack, that was his third M.I. He experienced his first cardiac episode at age 35!" Nicholas was stunned by this realization, having completely repressed this memory from his consciousness. This then allowed us to focus our therapy on Nicholas's unacknowledged, repressed, and unresolved trauma from the sudden loss of his father and his subsequent repressed fears of his own mortality. For Nicholas, approaching the age of his father's first heart attack set off an uncon-sciously driven panic reaction that manifested itself as an obsessive pur-suit of sex in an effort to ward off the specter of death.

Nicholas recalled continually thinking he, too, would die young and recalled that his father was not the only male in his family to experience an early demise. He also had two uncles and a cousin who died before their 40th birthdays. Death had stalked Nicholas from an early age, but he was unable to access and concede his fears to his conscious mind. His gritty, resolute, and tenacious repressive defenses protected him for many years until he essentially came face-to-face with his own mortality.

The result was a fanatical pursuit of a life force that would serve as an antidote to death, and that source of vitality was chased through sex.

Nicholas's case is noteworthy for several reasons. His clear recollection of when his problematic sexual behavior began is not so unusual. I have found that when dealing with problems such as these, sex therapists have not given enough attention to the timeline in which the behaviors began. Many of the patients I have treated with problematic sexual behavior have asserted that their behavior was not always uncontrollable for them. They would not always have described themselves as "sex addicts," having lived manageable, satisfying sexual lives prior to their confrontation with mortality. To me, that suggests that the timing of the onset of the difficulty is not only important but essential in understanding the message driving the sexual actions. It is my contention that some type of trauma, often an early childhood trauma, has been triggered, setting in motion an escalating and formidable series of actions. Most of the sex therapists who treat this type of condition focus their interventions primarily on stopping the problematic behavior rather than on understanding the function or meaning of the acting out. I have found that without an understanding of what the unconscious mind is trying to communicate through the man's penis and what dangers to existence the unconscious is attempting to protect the man from, any attempts to curb the behavior are temporary at best.

The next case is a bit different than the prior cases inasmuch as the primary losses in Marcus's life were of important and influential women. Marcus lived a childhood filled with multiple death traumas. Let's consider his story.

The Case of Marcus

Marcus was a 58-year-old man when he first presented for treatment. He was twice divorced but currently involved in a long-term relationship of 16 years' duration. Therapy was precipitated by his girlfriend, Bernadette's, discovery of a 12-year affair, as well as multiple one-night stands. Bernadette was threatening to leave the relationship, and Marcus was panicked. Both of his former wives left him after their discovery of his multiple infidelities. Marcus said he was afraid of being left again, even though he understood Bernadette's ire. He said he felt "compelled" to have these relationships, but he had no insight into what was driving his problematic sexual behavior. Of note is he met Bernadette during his recovery from a near-death automobile accident. She was an occupational therapist in the rehab hospital Marcus was being treated in, and he recalled she was instrumental in supporting him in his successful efforts to regain vital motor skills.

By way of history, Marcus was the oldest of six children. His mother died from breast cancer when he was 12 years old. His father remarried a year later and had two more children with his new wife. Marcus recalled being very close with his stepmother, as she was a warm, loving, and nurturing woman who treated him as if he was her biological child. Tragically, when Marcus was 19 years old, his stepmother also died from breast cancer. Marcus was devastated, as his stepmother was a much better caretaker and parent than was his father. Marcus's father was an alcoholic and died at age 57 from cirrhosis of the liver. Clearly, Marcus was visited by death many times as a youth. As a result, he reported that he was convinced that he too would suffer an early death.

For much of Marcus's life, he found himself involved with several women at the same time. In high school and college, girls would frequently break up with him upon the discovery of his sexual betrayals. He always felt driven to have multiple women in his life, even though he would most often have one primary relationship. He had little insight into why he felt compelled to have more than one woman but did report that it always felt crucial that he have options in case of a breakup. During his therapy, Marcus began to see that he was so terrified of loss that he felt compelled to have a substitute woman at the ready so he would never feel abandoned. Marcus suffered great fear of "running out": running out of time, running out of women, running out of potency. Much like Ebenezer Scrooge, Marcus was a "hoarder" of sorts. Recall that Scrooge collected money. He didn't spend it, he didn't enjoy it, he didn't share it, he just counted it as if he needed constant reassurance that he would have "enough." Scrooge also lost significant women in his life and likely protected himself from additional pain and suffering by shutting himself off from the rest of humankind. Marcus obviously did not shut himself off from others but clearly dreaded loss and abandonment. As a result, he made certain to always have a "spare" woman.

Marcus's story was filled with the trauma of early and unexpected death. The early demise of his mother, father, and stepmother set the stage for Marcus to believe that important life figures would disappear and leave him bereft of connection, nurturing, and love. It is not difficult to comprehend the anxiety Marcus suffered daily and how he would need to repress his insecurities in order to be able to function. Therapy for Marcus was successful, and he was able to repair the damage done to his relationship with Bernadette. A combination of individual and couples' therapy allowed Marcus to acknowledge his trauma-based insecurities, understand how his "hoarding" of women served an unconsciously driven self-protective function, and address the multiple death traumas and his resultant fears for his own mortality. Bernadette proved to be understanding and compassionate and was stirred to enter individual therapy to come to terms with her own early childhood trauma. I referred her to a colleague for her individual work, and both she and Marcus reported feeling like their lives and relationship had been reborn.

Let's now turn to a case that has a somewhat different twist. Recall Yalom's quote from his book *Staring at the Sun: Overcoming the Terror of Death* (2008), "While the physicality of death destroys us, the idea of death may save us" (p. 33). With this thought in mind, let me tell you about my patient, Gustav.

The Case of Gustav

Gustav was a 44-year-old married man who had been married to his wife for 22 years. He reported a pleasant, companionable, but unsatisfying marital life. In the years before Gustav's sexual problems came to the surface, he reported feeling increasingly "controlled" by his wife, saying his marriage had drained him of vitality. Additionally, he reported feeling like a "ghost" in his own house.

Gustav recalled being raised in a highly dysfunctional home. He assumed the role of mediator between his constantly warring parents and recalled frequent fears of death and loss. While he did not recall any early death experiences, he did report crying uncontrollably as a child, fearing that he was going to die. His preoccupation with death and fears of mortality continued into adulthood, but he had little awareness as to the source of his anxieties.

Approximately two years before our first meeting, Gustav's father-in-law died unexpectedly. During what was supposed to be a routine screening colonoscopy, Gustav's father-in-law had an unexpected allergic reaction to the anesthetic and died during the procedure. Gustav described this as a tremendous loss for him, as he felt closer and more connected to his father-in-law than he did to his own parents. His father-in-law was a mentor to him and relied on him often for advice and guidance. Gustav recalled becoming preoccupied with thoughts of "running out of time" and heightened fears of mortality following the traumatic death of his father-in-law. Monogamous to this point, Gustav felt propelled into a frenetic and chaotic pursuit of sex. He recalls feeling driven to "shock" himself and experience more than he had allowed himself thus far in this life. He reported an irrepressible need to "feel alive" and began a sexual spree that primarily focused on sex with men. Gustav reported these as his first same-gender sexual experiences. His sexual binge continued until his wife's discovery of his infidelities, although she was not aware that his extramarital sexual activities were with men. It was at this point that Gustav sought out psychotherapy/sex therapy. Note Gustav's use of the terms "vitality," "feel alive," and feeling like a "ghost in his own home." Such descriptions often signal a preoccupation with death and threats to one's existence.

Therapy for Gustav began by exploring his childhood and home environment. We then spent considerable time on his long-standing terror of death and fears of mortality. Gustav lamented never having been able to live the life he aspired to. While he was unclear about what that life would look like, he felt inspired to not allow himself to continue with such an unsatisfying existence. After a considerable time in therapy, Gustav revealed that once his sexual explosion calmed, he had been engaged in a continuous sexual relationship with a man he deeply loved. Gustav acknowledged that he was always sexually attracted to men but came from a family that openly derided homosexuality. His own internalized homophobia would not allow him to accept his genuine sexual urges, and he did all he could to repress them deep into his subconscious. The death of his father-in-law created an eruption in Gustav that broke through his repressive defenses and made him recognize that one's existence is both precious and precarious, and he would no longer deny his authentic self. Gustav had always felt his repressed sexuality was draining him of life's enthusiasm and energy, resulting in his "dying" inside. He resolutely vowed to himself that he was unable to continue with the disingenuous life he was living and was prepared to make substantial changes. His wife was surprisingly (to him) understanding, and while unhappy about the ending of her marriage and the disruption/betrayal to her life, she wanted him to be happy and her to have a relationship with someone who was sexually interested in her, and the marital dissolution was amicable.

Gustav's story is noteworthy because it represents the embodiment of Yalom's quote. By becoming aware of the inevitability of death and refusing to deny its specter, Gustav was able to courageously pursue a life that was meaningful, fulfilling, genuine, and authentic. The awareness of death saved him by inspiring him to no longer waste time in a false, meaningless, and unsatisfying existence. Had Gustav not finally acknowledged his true self, he would have ended his life with deep regret and remorse for a life unlived.

In each of the cases referenced in this chapter, the explosive change in sexual behavior appeared to be precipitated by an unexpected confrontation with mortality. For each of these men, their uncharacteristic, unpredictable, and insatiable sexual eruption represents an attempt to find vitality, solace, and a lifesaving energy force and to assuage fears of death. As their death terror persists, the behavior increases with a desperate intensity and surging frequency.

Traditional sex therapy for these conditions attends primarily to the sexual behavior itself and the need to curtail its upsurge. For the existential sex therapist, however, the focus is on what is driving the behavior and the need to mollify the existential terror of death that is causing this paroxysm of sexual conflict. Existential sex therapy contends that symptoms are often overdetermined and are expressions of attempts to defend the man from existential anxieties such as the terror of death. Therefore, treatment concentrates on finding the meaning, function, and message behind the symptom, as opposed to centering on the sexual behavior itself. Neither Donald, Nicholas, Marcus, or Gustav entered therapy with any notion of what was driving their actions, and it was only through the acknowledgment and subsequent awareness of the role the terror of death played in their lives that they were able to make the crucial changes vital for the restoration and/or creation of their life satisfaction and sexual behaviors.

Of course, not all cases of problematic sexual behavior are the result of the existential anxiety surrounding mortality. As James Cantor and colleagues (2013) mentioned at the beginning of this chapter, problematic sexual behavior is likely multidetermined, and there are multiple causes for such behavioral expressions. There is no one-size-fits-all treatment or explanation. However, a sole focus on the behavior without a thorough and in-depth analysis and understanding of the behavior is likely to result in a treatment that is incomplete and largely ineffective.

The type of problematic sexual behavior described in this chapter is often closely correlated with the core difficulty addressed in our next chapter, "Why Men Behave Badly." Certainly, the challenging sexual behavior discussed in this chapter could be described as "bad behavior," but many men display problematic expressions of sexual behavior. Noncompulsive infidelities, sex offenses, and the overly entitled transgressions of consent are but a few. While there is no debate about the fact that men often get themselves into sexual trouble, there has been little exploration of the "why" of this. Why sex? Why does much of men's bad behavior occur through their penis? Let's move to the next chapter and explore these phenomena in greater detail.

6

WHY MEN BEHAVE BADLY

Anthony Weiner. Eliot Spitzer. Andrew Cuomo. Louis C.K. Matt Lauer. Harvey Weinstein. Jeffrey Epstein. John Edwards. Bill Cosby. Charlie Rose. Kevin Spacey. Tiger Woods. There seems to be no end to the list of famous men who have seen their lives go up in flames due to their problematic sexual behavior. While most of what I know of these men comes from the same news reports that everyone else reads, I can't help but wonder what events in their lives may have shaped the trajectory of their sexual transgressions. Of course, this phenomenon is hardly limited to men who are well known, but these are the men whose problematic sexual behavior makes the headlines. Sex therapists can attest that bad sexual behavior is hardly limited to the rich and famous, but the behavior of men such as those listed here drives much of the narrative regarding how we understand and judge such egregious behavior.

The prevailing construal for men's odious and invasive sexual behavior is that men use sex to assert power, particularly over women, and use sex as a means for claiming authority, supremacy, and dominion over the weaker, more vulnerable members of society. While this portrayal

DOI: 10.4324/9781003127871-7

is a logical interpretation of offending men's behavior, it is notable that this depiction has largely been accepted with little examination, consideration, or question. Additionally, much of our current construction is reinforced by the academic field of "gender studies," which is comprised of a faculty the majority of which are women. A quick search of books on gender studies on Amazon.com reveals that the textbooks utilized are overwhelmingly authored by women. Furthermore, the gender breakdown in the mental health professions indicates that we are comprised of almost 70% identifying as women (Mental Health Worker, 2021; American Psychological Association, 2015)). Of course, this does not mean that women's interpretations of men's bad sexual behavior should be discounted, as women are most often on the receiving end of such affronts, but without input from men on their own problematic sexual behavior, our discernment of such activity is limited and incomplete. We are left with a predominant supposition that is little more than a picture based on a noncontextual, unnuanced snapshot of behavior. If simply observing the behavior of these men is going to be our manner of inquiry, then drawing such a conclusion about what drives bad sexual behavior makes sense. However, if we contemplate the context in which this behavior occurs, we very well may proffer alternative explanations.

To be clear: what follows in this chapter is an attempt to *explain* and better understand the egregious sexual behavior of men. It is NOT an attempt to postulate an excuse for such behavior. Those who behave badly must be willing to accept the consequences of their actions. While much of this offensive sexual behavior may be difficult to control due to a variety of medical or psychological ailments, we must recognize that it is the brain, not the penis, that is the primary driver of action (Willingham, 2020). A man's penis may be the conduit of expression, but it is brain that regulates behavior. That control mechanism may be compromised for myriad reasons, but it does not mean that men need not be accountable for their dubious behavior, and an understanding of that challenging phenomenon may aid in providing the needed intervention and treatment for assisting men to keep their insolent sexual urges in check.

So if men's invasive sexual behavior is not necessarily driven by the need to assert their power, what is driving such actions? Lisa Taddeo (2019), in her highly acclaimed book *Three Women*, is one of several women who challenge the male-power-and-dominance narrative. In discussing the sexual behavior of her father, Taddeo writes:

While I never had occasion to wonder about my father's desire, something in the force of it, in the force of all male desire, captivated me. Men did not merely want. Men needed . . . Presidents forfeit glory for blow jobs. Everything a man takes a lifetime to build he may gamble for a moment. I have never entirely subscribed to the theory that powerful men have such outsize egos that they cannot suppose they will ever be caught; rather, I think that the desire is so strong in the instant that everything else—family, home, career—melts down into a little liquid cooler and thinner than semen. Into nothing.

(pp. 3–4)

Taddeo advances the dialogue from a discussion of power to a consideration of desire. Her assessment is that a man's sexual desire is so strong that in the moment, he can be overcome by the need for sex. While I appreciate Taddeo's attempt to further the discourse and open the field for an exchange of ideas, I think she may be overstating the case for potent sexual desire as the driving force of such distasteful behavior. While this may be the case for some, let's consider some other possibilities.

Northwestern University professor Laura Kipnis, in her book *Men* (2014), makes several observations about powerful men who behaved badly. In discussing former presidential candidate John Edwards, she writes:

one of the more widespread explanations of Edwards' behavior was "hubris." This was shorthand for the view that Edwards was lying, knew he was lying, knew that exposure of his lies would mean downfall, thought he could get away with it, and simply miscalculated. Those who hew to this story are taking the position that all mental activity is conscious, and all facets of the mind are transparent to itself. Self-deception per se doesn't exist for this camp; those who engage in what might "look" like self-deception are actually fully conscious of what they're doing—they're "deliberately" acting badly and they know it; they're just hoping not to get caught.

(pp. 152–153)

Kipnis continues:

Opposing the hubris camp, we have what might be called the "compartmentalization" camp. Compartmentalization proponents would say that Edwards wasn't "consciously" deceiving his audience. He both knew what he was doing, and didn't: the main person he was deceiving was himself . . . Fooling yourself about the supremacy of self-knowledge makes you a walking example of compartmentalization.

(pp. 152–153)

Kipnis introduces two new twists to the power-and-dominance narrative. She suggests "hubris," or the idea that one can possess such an excessive self-confidence that they see themselves as being too clever to get caught or suffer any consequences for their actions. Her other notion is one of compartmentalization. Some men are apparently able to deceive themselves in such a manner that the driver of their behavior gets buried in the unconscious and allows the conscious mind to rationalize the offending behavior. John Edwards was the candidate who billed himself as the model "family man." He positioned himself as the ideal husband, doting father, and moral politician. Unfortunately, he was also cheating on his cancer-stricken wife, lied about it, changed the details, and then offered a weak mea culpa before ending his presidential campaign. To Kipnis, be it hubris or compartmentalization, men like John Edwards are anything but dullards. What they are is unaware or uncaring masters of self-deception. Bottom line—as in the words of Philip Roth's protagonist Alexander Portnoy, who when speaking to his psychiatrist, Dr. Spielvogel, utters the Yiddish phrase:

Ven der putz shteht, ligt der sechel in drerd. Know that famous proverb? When the prick stands up, the brains get buried in the ground!

(Roth, 1967, p. 128)

While power, desire, hubris, and self-deception may explain some of the motivations behind the poor sexual behavior of some men, other explanations have received far less consideration. I am of the opinion that many theorists and clinicians confuse the pursuit of power with the quest for vitality. In my experience, many of the men who act out sexually do so as the result of an existential crisis. While I have never met or evaluated any of the famous men listed above, I do know that Anthony Weiner encountered early, unexpected death when his 39-year-old brother died. Tiger Woods seemed to lose control of his sexual urges following the death of his father; Louis C.K.'s parents divorced when he was young, and he rarely saw his father after that; Harvey Weinstein's

father died young at age 52; John Edwards's wife, Elizabeth, was diagnosed with cancer at the young age of 55; Kevin Spacey and his siblings were reportedly repeatedly physically and sexually abused by their
father; and Bill Cosby had a brother who died tragically at age 6. Again,
while not excusing the behavior of any of them, is it possible that their
offending sexual behavior had some connection to a fear of mortality or
some other existential crisis?

Infidelity

By far the most frequently seen problematic sexual behavior in my practice is infidelity. While the betrayer is not always male, it is the unfaithful man who is overwhelmingly represented in my patient population.
While some men engage in extramarital affairs due to unhappiness or
a dissatisfaction with their marriage/relationship/partner, most of the
men I have worked with have no desire to end their relationships and
shatter their lives or the lives of their family members. So why do they
do it? This, of course, is often the principal looming question for their
partner, but it is also often perplexing to the men themselves. True, the
notions of power, desire, hubris, or self-deception are sometimes present, but these interpretations often do not resonate with my patients.
No, the preponderance of unfaithful men that I have worked with are
often suffering from a more existentially based crisis.

In her 2017 text *The State of Affairs: Rethinking Infidelity*, the acclaimed psychotherapist Esther Perel offers:

> *The one theme I hear above all else from those who have bitten into the forbidden apple
> is this: It makes them feel alive . . . The sense of aliveness is rarely the explicit motive
> for an affair—in many instances they don't quite know why it began—but it is often
> the unexpected meaning that is found there . . . Affairs are quintessential erotic plots in
> the ancient sense of eros as a life energy.*

(p. 173)

Perel continues:

> *In a surprising number of these cases, a direct line can be traced from an extramarital
> adventure back to our most basic human fear—the confrontation with mortality . . .*

When the grim reaper knocks at the door—a parent passes, a friend goes too soon, a baby is lost—the jolt of love and sex delivers a vital affirmation of life . . . Some people may have previously felt tempted, but I wonder if it is the brusque confrontation with the brevity of life and its fragility that emboldens them to seize the day and act. Suddenly they are unwilling to settle for a life half-lived. "Is this all there is?" They hunger for more . . . Maybe it is death with a capital D or maybe it is just the deadness that creeps up from dulling habit—whatever the case, I now see these affairs as a powerful antidote.

(pp. 174–175)

Similarly, Wilhelm Schmid (2015) opines on the prospect of aging and mortality:

As we get older, we witness the fount of our possibilities drying up. And so, with all our might we begin to protest: this can't have been it! Some think they can salvage their dwindling options by abandoning ongoing projects and ending existing relationships in order to start over one last time.

(p. 36)

Both Perel and Schmid have noticed the same basic phenomenon that I have been describing. So many of these men reference the feeling of aliveness, the closeness to death and the terrifying reminder of one's own mortality, and the recognition that sex often serves as a life force that offers the false promise of being the antidote to death. Let's look at a case example.

The Case of Franklin

Franklin was a 51-year-old married male when we had our first consultation. Therapy was precipitated by his wife's discovery of a long-term affair. Franklin, who had been married to his wife (Ellen) for 29 years, said he had been monogamous for 27 of those years before reconnecting with an old flame (Camilla) from college. Franklin expressed that he was unsure to why he sexually transgressed, since he deeply loved his wife and believed he was happily married. Certainly, their marriage had its difficulties, but overall, he felt satisfied. While at a business conference, he unexpectedly met up with his former girlfriend, and they struck up a conversation. Franklin recalled feeling a surge of aliveness when speaking to Camilla, a sensation he could not recall experiencing for quite a long time. They agreed to meet for dinner following the day's meetings, and Franklin left dinner that evening with a feeling of lightness and energy that he realized had been missing from his current life. They made plans to meet again for dinner the next evening, and that encounter culminated in a sexual reunion. Franklin recalled feeling intensely guilty the following day, but he couldn't resist the urge to see Camilla again. He was hungry to recapture that feeling of youthful exuberance, and Camilla, too, was similarly entranced. They continued to meet whenever possible, and both found the rekindled relationship to be exhilarating, enjoyable, and energizing.

Franklin was raised in a restrictive environment. Always a good student, he feared doing anything that would upset his parents. He recalls his parents as being two unhappy people living in a loveless marriage. Both seemed embittered by their disappointments in life and, as Franklin recollects, blamed the unfairness of the world for their fate. Franklin remembers feeling sad for his parents and determined to never live a life as empty as theirs. His overconcern with their despondency led Franklin to resolve that he would do his best to make them proud and hope to lift their desolation and misery, and this became his life's mission. Of course, Franklin was never able to achieve this goal, and he came to feel trapped in an existence that was determined by the wants and needs of others (recall our earlier discussion of isolation from the self). Franklin's own happiness never seemed to factor into his life's equation, and despite his best efforts and substantial successes, he recalls a childhood characterized by feelings of dejection and gloom.

Franklin left home for college, and his world changed dramatically. For the first time, he felt free to explore his own interests and desires without having his parents' misery in his face. He met Camilla, and they had a playful, exciting, and highly sexual connection. Their relationship lasted for about 8 months before they mutually agreed to move on, as their life goals appeared incompatible. Franklin wanted to be a physician with a busy, successful practice and to have a stable, loving marriage, and a houseful of kids. Camilla, on the other hand, wanted a life of adventure and travel. She didn't see herself settling down and certainly was uninterested in the prospect of having children as she saw them as an obstacle that would hold her back from the free-form life she envisioned for herself.

Approximately 3 months later, Franklin met Ellen while working a summer job. They hit it off immediately, and while Ellen was not as spontaneous and unstructured as Camilla, Franklin found her to be bright, levelheaded, sexy, and desirous of the same life plan as he. Their relationship blossomed, and they decided to marry shortly after Ellen's college graduation. At that time, Franklin was in his second year of medical school, and they both envisioned a bright future. Their first child came quickly and the second 14 months later. Unfortunately, their second child suffered from a rare neurological disorder that likely would produce a lifelong disability. They purchased a home, and Franklin began to feel the strain of managing his medical residency, a marriage, two kids (one with special needs), and a mortgage. Many of the old feelings of having too many people to please, along with the subordination of his own needs and freedom, led Franklin to experience a sense of despondency and the dread that he was descending into the lifeless, joyless existence of his parents.

As Franklin approached his 50th birthday, his sense of gloom and despair heightened. He feared he was missing too much of life and would die with the regret of never having fully lived. He wanted to place the blame on Ellen, the kids, his practice—anything that would remove the burden of having to hold himself accountable for the life he was living, or not living, as it were. It was shortly after this that he had the occasion to suddenly run into Camilla, and the memories of freedom, spontaneity, and vitality came flooding back to Franklin.

In Franklin's case, we see much of what Esther Perel and I have been noticing. Franklin's reaching the 50-year mark was a turning point for him ("0" birthdays can always be momentous. 40, 50, and 60 are critical milestones for many men). This was Franklin's confrontation with mortality. The fact that he lived much of his life with a progressive loss of vitality, energy, and joy generated a terror that he would spend the rest of his days in such a state. He wondered if there wasn't more to life than he was encountering. He wondered, should he make titanic changes to his life and start anew? His reunion with Camilla challenged his current melancholia by infusing him with an energy he had long forgotten. Ellen's discovery of Franklin's affair and her threat to end their marriage sent Franklin into a free fall of anxiety and panic and led to the beginning of his exploratory process via psychotherapy.

Therapy for Franklin began with an exploration of the current situation and his family of origin. Franklin was able to see how the circumstances of his adult life, while not at all unpleasant or problematic, triggered his childhood traumatic experiences of failure and isolation from self. Much of our work focused on acknowledging, understanding, and working through his traumatic childhood and how that childhood informed his adult life. As Alice Miller (1981) noted, Franklin was stuck in traumatic earlier life circumstances that, while once quite real, no longer existed.

Franklin was able to refute his inclination to follow the path of his parents and blame external factors for his anguish and assume the responsibility for being the one who creates his own life. Once able to accept this existential given, Franklin was able to make the necessary changes to his lifestyle and fashion an existence that minimized the regret of not fully living a life that was authentic, genuine, and satisfying. He was able to recognize the meaning of his rekindled desire for Camilla, and they ended their relationship amicably. Franklin and Ellen then began couples' therapy to repair the damage done to their relationship. Couples' therapy was productive, and Franklin and Ellen were able to reclaim the goodness in their relationship and construct a life that was fulfilling for both.

Let's look at another case of men behaving badly that was precipitated by a confrontation with mortality.

The Case of Eric

Eric was a 55-year-old male who presented for therapy after his wife's discovery of his extra-marital affair. Eric's wife, Marcia, had long suspected he was having an affair, but it wasn't confirmed until she saw romantic text messages on his phone. Eric was historically a private, guarded, and mistrustful man. He grew up with an ineffective yet abusive alcoholic father and an overinvolved and overcontrolling mother. As a young boy, Eric learned that the only way to avoid being overwhelmed by his mother was to cloak much of his life from her constant intrusion and surveillance. He would spend most of his time at home alone in his room and shared little of his life with his parents and older brother.

Academically and athletically accomplished, Eric would never share his triumphs (or occasional failures) with anyone in his family. He had many friends and was well liked but recalls being aware that he knew much more about his friends than any of them ever knew about him.

Eric dated often, but it wasn't until he met Marcia that he felt as if he'd met someone he imagined he could share a life with. Marcia was attractive, bright, upbeat, and fun, and she brought a vitality to Eric's life that he had heretofore found elusive. The couple married, moved into a nice neighborhood, had good, well-paying jobs, and, after a few years, began to have children. Eric and Marcia had two twin boys and, two years later, a daughter. Marcia was an extremely devoted mother. She doted on her children and gave up her career to be there to raise them in their younger years. She was happy and content with the life they had created, but Eric found himself becoming restless. As Marcia became more and more involved with the kids, Eric felt as though he was being shunted to the periphery of her life. This triggered in Eric the feelings of aloneness and isolation he felt from his childhood home, and he soon began to treat Marcia much like he had treated his mother. He became increasingly uncommunicative, spent more time alone in his study, and began coming home from work later and later, saying he had business functions to attend. Marcia, noticing the changes, tried several times to talk to Eric about what was happening, but he would just respond by saying that nothing was wrong, and he simply had a lot of business pressure.

At work, Eric had a female co-worker named Elaine who was personable, attractive, and clearly interested in him. In Elaine's presence, Eric again experienced the vitality that he had so enjoyed with Marcia, and the two of them began to lunch together, meet for after-work drinks, and eventually after-work dinners. A sexual relationship soon followed. Eric was unclear as to why he was pursuing the path he'd chosen, assuming it was merely because he felt ignored by Marcia. However, it soon became apparent that Eric was experiencing the triggering of an early childhood trauma that now threatened his life energy and his zestful spirit. Having to share Marcia's attention created a panic in Eric that the existence he had come to enjoy with Marcia was being jeopardized and vulnerable to loss. Never being comfortable with acknowledging or communicating his feelings, Eric swallowed his pain and suffered silently. Elaine reignited many of the feelings Eric was desperate to recoup, and he came to depend on Elaine for emotional sustenance and verve.

When Marcia discovered Eric's affair, she fully expected him to be remorseful, apologetic, and committed to repairing and restoring their marriage. Eric pledged to do so, but Marcia soon found evidence suggesting that Eric had not ended his relationship with Elaine. Naturally, Marcia was hurt and confused. She feared that she had lost Eric to another woman and had no idea what she had done wrong. Eric tried to reassure Marcia that she had, indeed, done nothing wrong and was a wonderful mother and supportive spouse. While Eric reported believing this fully, he found it impossible to renounce his relationship with Elaine. He was perplexed as to why this was so but discerned that letting go of Elaine created a despair in him that could not be easily suppressed. He saw Elaine as the key to his feeling energized and for his survival. He was, therefore, reluctant to release her and run the risk of going back to a life that was devoid of vivacity, animation, and vigor.

In therapy, Eric began to see the connection between his mode of controlling his mother's invasive behavior, his "lifeless" childhood, his vitality that emerged when he met Marcia, his triggered trauma when Marcia became so devoted to the kids, and the life energy he felt reappearing upon meeting Elaine. Individual therapy helped Eric better understand and manage his fears of returning to a life of deadness, and couples' therapy was of great benefit in restoring and revitalizing their marriage.

Yalom (2008) had a similar case in which a physician named Les married and moved into his new wife's home approximately 100 miles from where he was currently living. He opened a practice in his new community but maintained his old office, seeing patients there one and a half days a week. He would spend one night a week in his former community, connecting with old girlfriends. Les's death anxiety was somewhat different from Eric's in that Les feared that "closing doors" would be the death of his former life of freedom and choice. For many men, endings such as what Les was describing represent a form of death terror that drives them to keep the doors of sexual freedom and choice open.

As can be gleaned from the cases of Franklin, Eric, and Les, affairs are not always about relationship (or partner) dissatisfaction or about men wanting to exercise their narcissistic need for power and control over women. Certainly power, control, and partner unhappiness can be causes for extramarital affairs, but often, very often, infidelities represent something much more complex. For many men, extramarital affairs are the result of existential crises, and only awareness and acknowledgment of that fact are likely to lead the profound changes necessary to live a life of relational meaning, contentment, and happiness.

Sex Crimes and Offenses

Few groups of men are more maligned and vilified than those who commit sexual crimes and sex offenses. There is little debate about the substantial negative impact on victims of sexual assault and the fittingness of punishment for those who offend. Most sex offenders will spend a considerable amount of time in prison and then be subjected to long-term monitoring via Megan's Law. Few crimes are considered more heinous, and we tend to reserve much of our harshest criticism and chastisement for those who commit such actions.

However, sex crimes and offenses are also among those sexual behaviors that are most judged based on the behavior exhibited, with little attention or consideration given to what drives such problematic behavior. Historically, much of our treatment of such acts has been similar to that of the sexual addictions discussed in the previous chapter, in that our psychotherapeutic efforts have largely focused on behavioral interventions directed at stopping and controlling the behavior. The prevailing narrative has focused on the misogynistic male exercising power and control over women and children (Prescott et al., 2010). While this is undoubtedly the motivation for some sex crimes and offenses, other explanations deserve scrutiny as well.

Recall from earlier chapters our discussion of the work of Levenson et al. (2017). Levenson and her colleagues view much of sex offending through a trauma-informed lens. They assert that treatment aimed simply at stopping the offending behaviors without a consideration of possible early childhood trauma is likely to result in insufficient, incomplete, and ultimately ineffective therapy. Levenson and her colleagues have found that many of those men who commit sexual crimes and offenses have been severely traumatized themselves. Some have been victims of sexual assaults, and others have been subjected to other nonsexual horrific maltreatment from caretakers and/or authority figures. Levinson et al.'s treatment process recognizes the insidious nature and long-term impacts of early childhood trauma. Such a perspective helps to remind us that even those whose behavior is atrocious are still *people*, and all people can be victims of trauma. The hope is that by humanizing the offender and providing a compassionate trauma-informed treatment, the therapist can address the offender's own traumas, and rehabilitation will be successful.

Again, this does not excuse unacceptable behavior, nor does it negate the need for consequences. However, viewing such behaviors through a trauma-focused or trauma-informed lens may assist in determining what consequences are most appropriate and what treatments are likely to be most effective. Consider the following case presented by Levenson et al. (2017):

> Pete's mother was addicted to drugs and alcohol throughout the first years after her violent husband abandoned her and Pete. Unable to care for or protect him, she sent Pete to live with his uncle in another state and was in contact only sporadically throughout the rest of his childhood. Pete's uncle was physically and sexually abusive of him as well, especially when Pete did not complete his many chores on his uncle's farm. Pete learned over time to stand up to his uncle and developed the belief that whatever others might do to him he would have to do back to them threefold. Understandably, Pete developed the belief that the world is a dangerous and out-of-control place where two wrongs make a right.
>
> By the time he was 16, Pete had sexually abused two young boys in the neighborhood. Not surprisingly, his methods of abuse (e.g., forced fellatio and anal intercourse) were similar to what he had experienced himself. He was placed in a juvenile detention center where he was diagnosed with attention deficit/hyperactivity disorder (ADHD) and conduct disorder. At the time of his placement (the mid 1990's), these were considered such primary diagnoses that the various diagnosticians he encountered did not consider PTSD. Given his upbringing, Pete was not inclined to divulge sensitive information about himself. It was not simply that he did not trust the (mostly female) psychologists; the problem was that their presence invoked a combination of implicit beliefs about the world, including that people who might appear to care about him disappear and/or hurt him before long, and that one has to fight to stay safe. In this way, the treatment staff themselves activated the very response that made it unlikely he could engage in treatment.

According to Levenson et al., Pete did not do well in treatment. After his release at his 18th birthday, he lasted only a short time before he was again arrested for sexually assaulting a young boy. This arrest awakened Pete to the need to make changes in his life and provided the motivation needed to participate in and complete a treatment program. He viewed himself as a heterosexual and could not understand his behaviors.

Levenson et al. continue:

> A key problem that Pete faced was that every time he completed a treatment group session in the early phase of his program, he would return to his living unit only to be triggered by the uniformed staff who represented the power and authority that Pete had stood up to in order to survive. Importantly, it wasn't just that these staff reminded him of his uncle; it was that the very presence of this kind of authority activated a response that permeated his body as well as his mind, and his response to this authority was quicker than his reminder to himself that this would be a good time to use the cognitive skills he was learning about in treatment. By all appearances, Pete seemed to be on a direct route to multiple incarcerations and a diagnosis of antisocial personality disorder. Whatever his internal state of being, outside professionals saw only his overt aggression.
>
> (pp. 28–29)

Pete's case is noteworthy for several reasons. While Levenson et al. do not use the term "existential crisis," Pete clearly senses multiple threats to his existence: his mother's addiction and inability to care for and protect him, his father's abandonment, his mother's infrequent contact with him, the sexual abuse at the hands of his uncle, etc. It is little wonder that Pete came to view the world as a dangerous place and to be distrustful of those who were supposed to protect and care for him. From the time he was a young child, Pete learned that he needed to protect himself, and the notion of relying on authority figures for sustenance and protection only heightened his perception that he need be vigilant and prepared to strike first so as to fend off all potential threats to his existence and well-being. When viewed from an existential and trauma-informed lens, Pete's behavior shifts from the need to dominate and abuse to the need to protect the self. Pete's actions could easily be interpreted as the manifestation of an antisocial personality disorder, and as noted by Levenson and colleagues, early diagnosticians pronounced Pete as suffering from ADHD and conduct disorder. However, when considered within the contexts of Pete's life history, a diagnosis of PTSD seems more appropriate, and a treatment focused on the enduring impact of Pete's early childhood trauma and his subsequent use of sex as a source of strength and vitality as opposed to a treatment that aims to merely control his sexual behaviors offers much greater promise for healing and resolution.

Let's now turn to another type of sexual offending that sometimes manifests itself in men. Professional sexual misconduct, or the unacceptable sexual behavior of those professionals who are entrusted with the protection and well-being of the public, is a particularly egregious violation of civic trust.

Professional Sexual Misconduct

In addition to my psychotherapy work, I have also worked with many men whose behavior has either transgressed their profession's ethical standards or violated society's standard of law. While men who commit sexual boundary violations or sexual crimes are often vilified and maligned, it remains that these are still human beings whose behavior, while highly problematic and in need of sober consideration and often deserving of austere consequences, often operate for reasons other than evil, antisocial, or narcissistic impulses.

I place these professionals in one of two categories. The first are the predators. These are men who look to manipulate, abuse, and exploit their patients in order to satisfy their own selfish wants and desires. Fortunately, there are few who fall into this classification. By far the more common are those who are impaired or damaged by unexpected calamitous life circumstances. These are the professionals who may be experiencing financial troubles, marital/family/relationship difficulties, psychiatric illnesses, physical illnesses, substance abuse, etc. As a result, they severely mismanage the therapeutic relationship and often do great harm to their patients.[1] Such misfortune could visit any man and create an existential crisis that may result in uncharacteristic and aberrant sexual behavior. Consider the following case of a physician I evaluated for professional sexual misconduct. Allow me to introduce you to Carlos.

The Case of Carlos

Carlos was a 47-year-old, married physician who worked as a hospitalist in a large medical center. He had been employed in the same position for the past 17 years. Carlos was known as a competent, ethical, respectable member of the hospital's medical staff, and he was well liked by the hospital staff, including the attending physicians. Carlos was also known as a dedicated family man. He and his wife, Eva, were often described as a model for a great marriage. Carlos and Eva had three children, a daughter in college and two sons in high school. Both were actively involved in their kids' lives and spent much of their nonworking time taking family vacations, participating in PTA functions, and coaching youth sports teams. As a result, it came as quite a shock to all when Carlos was reported to the hospital administration for allegations of sexual misconduct.

Carlos had recently begun initiating sexually provocative conversations with some of the nursing staff in the intensive care unit and was exposing his penis to several of the women working on the unit. At first, there was a reluctance to report Carlos since he was so well liked and respected, and this behavior seemed so out of character for him. However, as his behavior persisted, staff felt as if they had no choice but to alert the medical center's administration. Carlos was suspended to allow for an investigation, and the allegations were found to be credible. Carlos was then put on leave pending a psychiatric evaluation. Such was the precipitant for the referral to me.

At our first meeting, Carlos expressed great remorse and embarrassment for his sexually offensive actions. This behavior represented an aberration of Carlos's general manner, and he was at a loss to explain what was driving his uncharacteristic sexual behavior. He had never behaved this way before recent weeks and felt great shame at having his and his family's reputation tarnished. He did admit to being under a great deal of stress in the past several months but did not see a connection between his recent sexual acts and his nonsexual anxieties.

Carlos was unable to place his problematic sexual behaviors in any context that made sense to him. However, Carlos had been spending particularly long hours tending to patients in the intensive care unit during the early months of the COVID-19 pandemic. People were dying all around him from an illness that was poorly understood and, as a result, being treated in a muddled, confused, and frenzied mode. People, including healthcare professionals, were unnerved, frightened, overworked, and exhausted. Scientists and government officials were giving ever-changing messages about the virus, and the specter of death ruled the day. Carlos reported coming home at the end of the day haunted by feelings of terror and dread and would spend much of the evening crying. He had been awakened by chilling nightmares of people being tortured, tormented, and suffering. His sleep quality was deteriorating by the week, and Carlos reported getting up each day and going back to the ICU feeling like a "zombie." He recalls that the day before his first sexual transgression, he was tending to a patient who happened to be the 45-year-old wife of his best friend. Her health was deteriorating rapidly, and he watched her have a final conversation with her husband and children via a laptop computer.[2] Carlos could not help but think that that could have easily been him and his wife, and the death of his best friend's wife brought death uncomfortably close.

While context eluded Carlos, it was clear to me that Carlos was experiencing an acute case of death terror. He was inundated with the reality of death's intrusion at every turn. While he was an experienced ICU physician, the cloud of death overwhelmed Carlos's typically strong death defenses, and he began to crumble. As was the case with so many of the men we have discussed, Carlos unconsciously turned to sex, the life force, hoping for a reprieve from the menacing shadow of death. Carlos was far from alone in his mortality/sex connection during this period. I have many physician patients who have experienced an uncharacteristic sexual disruption in the face of the COVID-19 pandemic—otherwise monogamous men who were now having affairs, going to massage parlors, seeking out sex workers, spending hours looking for novel types of pornography, masturbating more frequently and often in the bathrooms or on-call rooms in the hospital. Each of these men was terrified by the dark veil of death that surrounded their lives. Each of these men turned to sex in a futile attempt to find an antidote to the overpowering presence of death. Fortunately, a therapy that focused on the meaning of the sexual behavior, their terror of death, and the self-protective function of the unconscious was able to assist these men with dealing more effectively with the horrors they had to encounter daily.

In this chapter, we examined through an existential lens some of the reasons men engage in problematic, abusive, and offensive sexual behavior. The prevailing narrative of power, control, narcissism, and hubris, while sometimes correct, has essentially escaped close inspection and scrutiny. Sexually transgressive behavior has primarily been judged on its face rather than an analysis of what drives that behavior and, thus, the meaning behind that behavior. In this chapter, we once again see the specter of death and the fear of mortality triggering a self-protective sexual response in the desperation to find an antidote to human demise. Sex, the life force, is again called upon to assuage the fear and horror that overpowers otherwise responsible and respectful men. Keeping this in mind may assist us in providing effective treatment and appropriate consequences for those men whose sexual actions trespass on the lives of others.

Our final chapter will look at the dilemmas and existential crises faced by aging men. These are men for whom the shadow of death is not far in front of them. Let's look at how aging and sex can be understood through an existential lens.

Notes

1. For an excellent discussion of sexual and boundary violations and their impact on the therapeutic relationship, please see Jeffrey Berman and Paul Mosher's text, *Off the Tracks: Cautionary Tales About the Derailing of Mental Health Care, Vol. 1: Sexual and Nonsexual Boundary Violations.*
2. In an effort to contain the spread of the COVID-19 virus, patients were not allowed to have any in-person visitors no matter how dire their condition. As a result, many hospitalized COVID patients died without being able to spend their last months, weeks, days, hours, or minutes with loved ones.

7

AGING

The Penis Speaks,
but Sometimes It Whispers

We are getting older. That is both the good news and the bad news (at least for some of us). Aging means we are still alive and presented with the opportunities to live life well. On the other hand, each passing day brings us a bit closer to the finish line. While this is how it must be, many of us will do all we can to keep a distance between our lives and the end.

Truth is, most of us do not look forward to aging. We live in a culture that prizes youth and treats aging as if it were a disease. Most of our images of aging men are filled with negativity, loss, and fears of irrelevance. The unfortunate result is that many of us will pursue the ever-elusive image of youth rather than accept the fact that the life cycle is always moving forward and we need to adjust and accommodate its changes. Barbara Ehrenreich, in her book *Natural Causes: An Epidemic of Wellness, the Certainly of Dying, and Killing Ourselves to Live Longer* (2018), laments the fact that we portray "successful aging" as maintaining our youthful appearance and vigor. Indeed, she points out that those over 55 years of age account for the fastest-growing demographic for new gym memberships. Of course, it is widely and wisely acknowledged that regular

DOI: 10.4324/9781003127871-8

exercise is an important component of healthy living, but Ehrenreich opines that it is not the quest for good health that drives the aging to gyms; rather, it is the quest for a youthful appearance.

In an article from the *New York Times* (2011), Ellin reports on the escalation of cosmetic surgeries for Americans over the age of 65. She reports that according to the American Society for Aesthetic Plastic Surgery, in 2010, there were close to 85,000 cosmetic surgical procedures among patients age 65 and older. This includes almost 27,000 face-lifts, almost 25,000 cosmetic eyelid operations, almost 7,000 liposuctions, just under 6,000 breast reductions, more than 3,500 forehead-lifts, over 3,000 breast-lifts, and almost 2,500 breast augmentations. While it should be no one's business if people over the age of 65 choose to cosmetically augment their appearance, many bioethicists have expressed concern that such purely cosmetic procedures for the aging may represent a collusive yet unacknowledged effort between physicians and patients to deny the reality of the aging process (Watter, 2012). Indeed, current efforts have suggested reaching beyond what is "age-defying" to the pursuit of that which is "age-reversing." Sifferlin (2018) reported on a group of researchers who are investigating the potential benefits of nicotinamide adenine dinucleotide, or NAD+, as an antiaging therapy that will extend life indefinitely. Others, such as Nir Barzilai, M.D., the director of the Institute for Aging Research at New York's Albert Einstein College of Medicine, have been investigating the use of the popular diabetes drug Metformin to assess its ability to prevent the onset of certain age-related diseases and thereby delay and defy death. Barzilai's goal is to persuade the FDA to designate aging as a treatable condition and Metformin as a drug that can effectively stop or at least substantially slow the aging process (Hall, 2015).

Such efforts may infiltrate the sex therapy field in that many of our interventions and attitudes promote a vision of sexuality and aging that is heavily slanted toward the maintenance or restoration of the sexual functioning of youth, as opposed to assisting our aging male patients with the development of a greater acceptance of the realities of life-stage changes and a greater enjoyment of the natural bodily changes that accompany the aging process. We continue to encourage firm erections for our male patients, whether by using oral medications, testosterone patches or injections, penile injections, vacuum pumps, or surgically implanted penile prostheses. Again, for those men who wish to pursue such options, there should be no judgement. But as sex therapists and sexual medicine physicians, are we really doing our patients a service by promoting the pursuit of youthful sexual function? Would we not be of greater assistance if we were more positive and encouraging of the discovery of a sexual life that is more suited to the later stages of life? I'm sure that by now, you know where I stand on this. We chase the sexual function of youth because we are attempting to run away from death. Aging represents an existential threat to existence that will not be overcome. While some are researching that which essentially constitutes a never-ending life and the prize of immortality, today's reality is that death will eventually find us, and any attempts to refute that certainty are little more than an active state of denial.

While we know that there are bodily changes that will impact men's sexual functioning as they age (decreased frequency of morning erections, decreases in penile sensitivity, slower-occurring erections, the need for more penile stimulation, less rigid erections, reduced ejaculatory urgency/intensity/consistency/volume, longer refractory periods, and more rapid postejaculation detumescence), so long as they are reasonably healthy, the importance of sex remains for many. Indeed, even if we are not so healthy, the importance of sensual human contact endures. Consider the words of Schmid (2015) when describing the significance of touch.

> When I am being touched, I am alive and feel that I am alive. When I am no longer touched, life eludes me, I no longer feel it . . . But precisely as our need for touch increases, others' willingness to touch us decreases. Our skin no longer invites being touched, as when we were babies . . . The truth is: our culture, which promotes and idolizes the fragrant and unblemished complexion, turns old people into "untouchables," as though touching them would lead to "contracting" old age and, consequently death.
>
> (pp. 82–83)

Let's look at these musings in greater detail.

Aging and Male Sexuality

Despite the rapid growth of our aging population, we know little about their sexuality (Lindau et al., 2007). Our research on sex and aging has largely reinforced the erroneous notion that aging's effect on sexual function results in an inevitable decline that will ultimately impede one's enjoyment of sex (Agronin, 2014; Bouman & Kleinplatz, 2016). This is likely due to the fact that our research on sex and aging is meager and tends to conflate aging with disease (Bouman & Kleinplatz, 2016). The result is that much of our data on sex and aging comes from the notion that the aged are a single cohort, and little consideration has been given to health status, cultural and/or religious differences, and age variance in what is actually a highly diverse and heterogenous group. Bouman and Kleinplatz (2016) also assert that most of our professional literature on aging and sexuality has concentrated on topics such as sex in residential and nursing home settings, sex and illness/disability, sexuality and dementia, disinhibited sexual behavior, and other topics related to aging and impairment. Additionally and perhaps most noteworthy is that most of our studies have concerned themselves with the presence or absence of *coital* activity and the absence or difficulty with sexual intercourse. Such focus has led to the conclusion that the overwhelming majority of aging adults suffer from sexual dysfunction and a lack of sexual happiness and satisfaction.

While we know that men's sexual health and sexual functioning can be compromised for many reasons, health and otherwise, Kontula and Haavio-Mannila (2009) have reported that even though many older men acknowledge experiencing chronic health conditions, such conditions are rarely cited as barriers to *sexual enjoyment*. Indeed, some studies have suggested that as many as three-quarters of our aging population report satisfying and enjoyable sex lives (University of Michigan, 2018). Furthermore, Lindau et al. (2007) and Stulhoffer et al. (2018) report that the majority of older adults in their samples consider sexuality to be an important part of their lives.

How, then, are we to understand this seeming contradiction? If so many men are experiencing difficulty with sexual functioning, how could they be satisfied? It would appear that sexual satisfaction in aging men is not as tied to youthful functioning as we may have been led to believe. Perhaps, as mentioned earlier in this book, those who live well age well, and that allows these men to accept their changes in sexual function and not fear death so long as their relational lives have been strong.

We need to recognize that for many aging men, sex is still important, but their expectations of what sex is "supposed" to look like may have evolved to a sexuality that is consistent with the normal bodily changes of aging. That would suggest that as men age, they come to value other venues for sexual fulfillment and the feeling of "aliveness" more highly than the penetrative sex of youth.

But of course, these are not the men we are most likely to see in our practices. The men we see are those that insist that life be a never-ending upward spiral. Any assault on their physical being is treated as an aberration instead of an expected reality. These men do all that is within their power to thwart (deny) the inevitability of physical decline and the irreversibility of the passage of time. Take the case of Samuel, for example.

The Case of Samuel

Samuel was a 67-year-old man who had come to see me five years after his radical prostatectomy. He and his partner, Greg, had been together in a serious committed relationship for over 30 years. Samuel was stunned when he received his diagnosis of prostate cancer but chose an optimistic (perhaps overly optimistic) view, believing that his erectile abilities would be minimally impacted by the surgical removal of his prostate. Unfortunately, five years after surgery, he was having negligeable penile responsiveness and continued urinary leakage. Samuel had reluctantly tried oral medications without much success and found penile injections to be intrusive, uncomfortable, and unsatisfying. Due to his continued erectile difficulties, Samuel found himself withdrawing from Greg sexually and affectionately and shared little of his thoughts and feelings. When queried about his apparent detachment from Greg, Samuel's response was, "Why start something I can't finish?"

Clearly, Samuel was suffering from feelings of embarrassment and frustration, and his reaction was creating tremendous distress in his relationship with Greg. Samuel was angry that he wasn't one of the fortunate men to undergo surgical treatment for prostate cancer and emerge with his erectile ability relatively unimpaired. Greg was understanding of Samuel's distress and tried to offer a view of sex that was less erection focused. He tried to remind Samuel of how much fun sex was when they were first dating and waiting to have penetrative sex. Greg recalled the fun and enjoyment of oral sex and mutual masturbation and tried to frame it as a "journey back in time." Samuel was not persuaded and with disdain replied, "I don't want to go back to having sex like an adolescent." "Yes, but we had such fun back then," Greg reminded him. Samuel looked away with contempt and replied, "Yes, but back then, there was the anticipation that we were going somewhere. Now we are going nowhere."

For Samuel, the loss of erectile functioning precipitated an existential crisis, making him feel as if his life energy was slipping away. He described a loss of vitality and a march toward death. Therapy with Samuel consisted of a deep exploration of his fears of death, illness, debilitation/impairment, and the loss of the intimate connection he enjoyed with Greg. Once these concerns were acknowledged and addressed, Samuel was able to open up and be more receptive to nonpenetrative sexual options. At last contact, Samuel and Greg reported doing well and profoundly enjoying their "altered" sexual connection.

Samuel's situation was noteworthy in that he was experiencing what Sagar (2018) refers to as a *resentment* of death. Sagar suggests that some men resent illness and death, as it represents an assault on our personal agency. No one asks for prostate cancer, or any other illness for that matter, and some will experience this loss of agency as a personal affront— as an entity that robs us of time and vitality before we are ready to let them go. Sagar intimates that the desire for immortality is not simply about the desire to live forever but rather the desire to choose and control when life and sexual functioning will end. Of course, we often do not get that choice, and in Samuel's case, the loss of personal agency and the anger surrounding that loss were unmistakable, as was its precipitation of an existential crisis.

Another interesting feature of Samuel's case is that it demonstrates that unlike in earlier chapters, where a triggering of early childhood trauma set off an existential crisis that results in a sexual shutdown, many of our aging male patients see aging and illness themselves triggering an existential crisis that is often not rooted in early childhood experiences. Samuel experienced what Parkes (1975) refers to an assault on his "assumptive world." According to Parkes, our assumptive world consists of those beliefs that comprise an individual's view of reality. Humans hold strongly held assumptions about the world and the self that are learned over time and confirmed by many years of life experience. Severe stress and trauma provide challenges to our assumptive world in the form of rendering our understanding of the world, particularly our existential world, obsolete. The result is often a desperate fight to maintain the world as we know it. In discussing the plight of a man who has unexpectedly lost his sight, Parkes writes:

> Only if he can be brought to examine the extent of his incapacity and to grieve for the world which he must give up will he be prepared to learn the use of cane, braille, typewriter, guide dog, etc., which, between them, can help him to achieve reasonable self-reliance and to build a new and worthwhile assumptive world to live in.
>
> This example illustrates very clearly a common problem of psychosocial transition, the tendency to maintain the "status quo" at all costs and avoid learning the tasks appropriate to a new unwanted world. Those who are in a position to give support and guidance at such times must be prepared to assist the other person to examine his assumptions, to clarify the model of the world which predated the transition and the situation which now obtains in order to discover which aspects of it must change and which aspects can be retained.
>
> (p. 136)

Parkes, although not addressing sexual function specifically, echoes much of the main premise of this book. Compromised penile functioning forces a man to reconsider and reconfigure his assumptive world. It goes well beyond the mere ability to have sex. In an existential sense, the loss of penile functioning coerces a man to deal with a perceived threat to his existence inasmuch as he now finds his basic identity as a man and as a human being questioned. Essentially, what creates such panic and drives men with problematic penile functioning to go to such lengths to restore penile rigidity is not simply the preservation of his *sexual* ability; rather, it is about the conservation and perpetuation of his assumptive world, which is now jeopardized by the intrusion of an unwanted and oftentimes resented world which threatens to replace it.

For many men who have reached the end of their lives with deep regret for a life not well lived and with the unrealistic expectation that loss, illness, injury, or death remain lodged in the distant future, the realization that they are running out of time results in an existential panic. This panic, then, becomes the focus of the treatment.

Is the Quest for Meaningful Sex and Connection in Old Age Realistic?

Can sex actually be enjoyable or even (gasp!) better as we age? Well, it depends (no, this is not a joke about adult diapers!). So what does it depend upon? Existentially speaking, those of us who have lived well will also age well. If we have lived a life of meaning and connection, we will be more accepting of the changes that accompany the aging process and be more receptive to the accommodations that must be made in order to continue to live an existence of sexual satisfaction and fulfillment.

For some, aging brings with it a certain comfort and contentment, as life can be experienced as less stressful and pressured. Menard et al. (2016) have suggested that older adulthood may be a time of sexual growth and heightened enjoyment. Ehrenreich (2018) boldly asserts that in later life, she has found a refreshing refusal to take on every potential obligation or opportunity, to enjoy a decline in ambition and competitiveness. McCarthy and Metz (2007) advocate a certain sexual "wisdom" that comes with maturity and a greater awareness and comfort with our bodies. And Leiblum and Sachs (2002) describe a woman who had become much more open and freer in her sexual expression once reaching age 75. She reported a lessening concern with other's opinions or judgments of her and a greater ease with herself and sexual expression. Sachs and Leiblum report an older female clinician describing sex in later life to them as being different than the sex of youth but no less enjoyable. She says:

> Sex when you're younger is like downhill skiing—you get towed up to the top of this mountain and then, whoosh, you come straight down. But sex when you're older is like cross-country skiing. You get to take your time, see the scenery. It takes time to enjoy yourself, but in highlife, you've got a lot of time. You may be retired, or at least not tied to any schedule, and you can make love whenever you choose.
>
> (p. 129)

Several sex therapy clinicians have offered views of sex and aging that are both positive and realistic. Unfortunately, many more have offered prospects that are unrealistic and, in the end, destructive. The market is flooded with books, magazine articles, and internet posts promising the restoration of the sexual vitality of youth. Their claim is that there is no need to settle for a "limited" sexual life, and the changes brought on by aging can be overcome or, better yet, cured. Sadly, many Americans buy into the conflation of aging with disease and will follow a potentially damaging and disappointing path toward the "alleviation" of the vicissitudes of aging. For many men, the acceptance of the aging process is seen as giving in to weakness. In reality, it is an awareness of the inescapable decline of human function. The refusal to acknowledge and submit to the physical and sexual changes inherent in the aging process amounts to no more than a denial of the bounds of human existence. The truth, while difficult for some to admit, is that this decline is precisely what is *supposed* to happen. There is a reason why we refer to human existence as a "life cycle." A life is not supposed to last forever, and those who refute this certainty in the futile pursuit of youth are wasting the precious gift of time and life.

There are, however, some sex therapy clinicians who have offered realistic, positive, and helpful suggestions for maintaining a satisfying sex life in aging. Barry McCarthy and the late Michael Metz (McCarthy & Metz, 2007; Metz & McCarthy, 2007) have been stout and persuasive proponents of our ability to enjoy sex well into our 80s and beyond. They advocate for an acceptance of our bodies as they change as opposed to a fight against the natural aging process. They offer their "good-enough sex" model, which focuses on enjoying the sex our bodies give us rather than insisting on self-defeating performance expectations. They maintain that good sex is about acceptance, pleasure, and realistic potentials. In the good-enough sex model, intimacy, satisfaction, and pleasure are the goals of sexual behavior, and individuals and couples are encouraged to find their own unique sexual style that reflects the actualities of their changing bodies. The key to finding sexual pleasure in our older years is the willingness to grow and be creative, flexible, and curious.

Psychologist and sex therapist Peggy Kleinplatz (2010) has observed that among her aging patients, those who are present in the moment, authentic, communicative, connected, intimate, and willing to be vulnerable and take risks often find sex to be extraordinarily satisfying. Kleinplatz (2010) and Menard et al. (2016) both agree that when working with those who are struggling to adjust to bodily and sexual changes in later life, sex therapists can be most helpful by encouraging patients to let go of many of the conventional ideas about how sex is "supposed" to be and assist them in discovering new paths toward sexual enjoyment and fulfillment. Menard et al. add that central to individuals and couples finding sexual satisfaction in later life are active pursuit and receptive openness to experience.

Through the years, many sex therapists have encouraged their patients to be accepting of the realities of changing bodies and to be less goal oriented in their sexual behavior. However, patients have often resisted such propositions and insisted that if they couldn't have the sex they wanted (i.e., the sex of youth), they would rather have no sex at all.

Remember the case of Samuel from earlier in this chapter. Samuel was initially unwilling to accept the notion that sex can be enjoyable without a firm penis. Samuel was furious that he had to deal with the sexual complications resulting from his prostate cancer surgery. He cursed his doctors, cancer, God, and basically every other entity he could think of. Indeed, when I first met him, he was angry at psychology and sex therapy for not being able to provide him with a solution to his infirmity. I was the third therapist Samuel consulted. His prior therapists tried all of the standard sex therapy interventions, both medical and psychological. The urologists offered oral meds, penile injections, and vacuum devices. The mental health professionals recommended sensate focus, disputed irrational cognitions, meditation and/or mindfulness, and provided encouraging words in long line of unsuccessful efforts to get Samuel to renounce the notion that a hard penis was a prerequisite for satisfying sex. His visit to me was made with a fair amount of trepidation, skepticism, and hostility.

One of the unfortunate gaps in the sex therapy literature is the provision of guidance as to how to deal with and overcome this common resistance. I believe sex therapy has had little to say about the resistance presented by our elderly patients (or younger patients dealing with injuries or illnesses that impair sexual function) because as a field, we have fallen prey to the lure of the cherishing of youth. Many of us in the sex therapy field join with our patients in the elusive search for youthful penises and vaginas. Even those of us who try to provide our aging patients with accurate psychoeducation or the development of new sexual scripts report little success in their attempts to shift our patients toward a more age-appropriate and realistic view of sexual function. It is my assertion that the answers to this conundrum will be found outside of the sex therapy literature. Much of our treatment neglects to adequately deal with the anger and frustration associated with loss of function and the omnipresent existential dilemmas that chaperone us through the aging process.

The Existential Dilemmas of Aging

Like it or not, aging is a process that is defined by loss. Of course, this is not to suggest that our aging years cannot be enjoyable and fulfilling, but we are confronted with loss in a manner that no other stage of the life cycle proffers. As we age, we lose friends, relatives, and loved ones to death at a rate that some describe as terrifying. We lose many of our physical abilities and may have to give up many of the symbols of our autonomy (i.e., driving, living independently, etc.). Some of us will have to end careers that formed a large part of our identity. The list of losses is long, varied, and goes on and on. Many will find this a most unsettling realization. In his novel *The Dying Animal*, the novelist Philip Roth (2001) writes:

> Can you imagine old age? Of course you can't. I didn't. I couldn't. I had no idea what it was like. Not even a false image—no image. And nobody wants anything else. Nobody wants to face any of this before he has to. How is it all going to turn out? Obtuseness is de rigueur.
>
> (p. 35)

Roth painfully laments the changes that come with aging and his feeling unprepared to navigate this stage of life. He expresses the agony of arriving at the realization that his unwillingness to imagine aging and eventual demise was no more than a thinly veiled denial of the effect of time moving forward. One senses the anger and frustration that stem from the assault on his personal agency—the sense that the end of life has been unfair, and he should have received a more favorable ruling. You can almost hear the words of Dylan Thomas (1957) screaming out of both Samuel and Roth, "Rage, rage against the dying of the light." A therapy that doesn't deeply address the fuming wrath that accompanies loss is unlikely to be effective in fostering an acceptance of what is and the crucial receptivity to change.

From an existential perspective, losses such as those mentioned represent the ultimate threat to one's existence. Existential therapists such as Erik Erikson (1963) have noted that if one has not lived well, one will not age well. Erikson describes in his eighth and final stage of psychosocial development the arrival of the crisis of integrity versus despair. This stage of development begins at age 65 and ends at death. According to Erikson, the successful resolution of this crisis (i.e., integrity) is achieved only if one believes that he has lived a life that has been meaningful and satisfying. If integrity is not realized, despair over a life lived with significant regret will be the consequence. Existential psychotherapists Rollo May (1953) and, of course, Irv Yalom (1980) have echoed these same sentiments. Those who have not lived well will likely suffer the greatest distress over aging and changing bodies. They will fear the creep toward death and the regret of lost time and struggle mightily to navigate the challenges of aging and compromised sexual functioning. If we accept the notion that living well is consistent with aging well, it would suggest that sex therapy with our aging patients needs to focus on the emotions of distress, anger, fear, regret, and loss. To ignore or give short shrift to these often-painful conditions will likely produce ineffective and unsatisfying therapy.

Shaw (2001), claims that practicing sex therapy with the mindset of sex being either functional or dysfunctional based solely on physical abilities does a disservice to our patients. She suggests a frame adjustment that emphasizes the *meaning* of sex and how that significance is reflected in our lives and relationships as being much more impactful than a therapy that is focused on the "mechanics." Shaw's suggestions are consistent with the central beliefs of existential psychotherapy and existential sex therapy that meaningfulness comes from being connected to others relationally and that it is the engagement in deep, consequential relationships that is most likely to result in a successful resolution of Erikson's integrity-versus-despair crisis. Those who are able to effectively navigate the existential crises of aging are those most likely to be open to allowing themselves to be vulnerable, receptive, and willing to take the risks of allowing the past to be our past while reveling in the discovery of new and different sexual scripts that lie ahead. If we are able to effectively do our jobs as sex therapists, our patients will experience an adventure that will be perceived as being exhilarating, rejuvenating, and life affirming. Let's take a look at another case.

The Case of Harold

The case of Harold is one that I have presented a version of in a previous publication (Watter, 2020). I am bringing it back here because it is a case of an older male replete with existential themes.

Harold was an 82-year-old widowed man who presented for treatment after being referred by his urologist. Harold's primary complaint was that he was noticing decreased penile sensitivity that resulted in a less pleasurable orgasm. In addition, Harold complained that it would sometimes take up to an hour of masturbation to reach climax. At the time of referral, Harold had no partnered sexual activity. His wife of almost 50 years, Jocelyn, had passed away the year before, but they had not had any partnered sexual activity for the last 40 years of their marriage. According to Harold, neither seemed to enjoy partnered sex, and he derived a great deal of pleasure from solitary masturbation. His enjoyment and interest in solitary masturbation continued until this past year.

At first glance, I found Harold's presentation surprising. It seemed obvious that an 82-year-old man should, indeed, be experiencing reduced penile sensation and a longer time to reach orgasm. I had expected he probably had some difficulty with erections as well, but Harold said that erections were fairly easy to achieve and maintain. I assumed that much of our work would consist of some basic sex education about the normal sexual changes that an aging body will experience and/or some unresolved grief about the death of Jocelyn, but something told me to hold my tongue and ask him more about his life.

Harold recalled always being an "odd" person. He was never socially comfortable and believed he always struggled to pick up social cues. His childhood was traumatic, and he feared both his mother and father. His parents divorced when he was 11 years old, and he recalls he was a "neglected" and lonely child. He did have an older brother, but his brother was quite cruel and abusive. Harold felt like much of his life had been a disappointment.

He was Ivy League educated, including a doctoral degree in English literature. Harold hungered for a university faculty appointment, but at the time he was looking, positions in English literature were few and far between. With a poor job market and his inadequate social skills, Harold was unable to obtain the employment he desperately wanted. He settled for a job in a library that allowed him to surround himself with the books he loved but considered the position far below what he had envisioned for himself.

Harold met Jocelyn in graduate school, and they married after two years of dating. He reported enjoying married life very much. Although the relationship was minimally sexual, he enjoyed pleasing Jocelyn in nonsexual areas, and she seemed to appreciate him as well. The couple enjoyed reading, visiting museums, and attending chamber music concerts. These are activities Harold had enjoyed doing solo before meeting Jocelyn, and he continued to delight in them even after her death. During Jocelyn's extended illness, Harold took great pleasure in being her caretaker and felt as if he had little to occupy his time since Jocelyn's death. Indeed, Harold reported becoming increasingly distressed about the prospect of his own mortality following the death of Jocelyn. The couple had two children, both now grown, and both resided several states away from Harold. He reported having a positive relationship with each of the children, but neither required much of Harold. They would not see each other often but would speak by telephone on a weekly basis.

At our second session, Harold revealed his infatuation with a 15-year-old girl, who was the daughter of a family friend. Harold spoke of her in romanticized, loving, yet nonsexual terms. He loved sending her poems, music, and books he imagined she would be interested in. She would voice appreciation for these gifts, but Harold was frustrated by her seeming lack of enthusiasm for his guidance in life matters. This was not the first time Harold had experienced such frustration. He often found himself enamored by older adolescent/young adult females and would excitedly try to interest them in his cultural pursuits. Unfortunately, for Harold, while most of the girls were polite and gracious, none ever reciprocated his attentiveness.

Initially, my concern that Harold might be expressing pedophilic/hebephilic urges was activated. I wondered where he was going with this but soon realized that his interests in young girls was not sexual but more reflective of his desires to "teach" and guide young people to the classics. Harold always saw his worth and meaning being rooted in the realm of giving to others, and he remained perplexed as to why the young girls who seemed so nice to him were so uninterested in his literary and musical pursuits. He felt he has so much to give, and much like his frustration from not being able to find a place in the life of an academic, Harold was similarly vexed by the lukewarm reception his tutelage received.

Harold spent an entire session showing me pictures of his family of origin. His narratives were filled with stories of loneliness, neglect, parental fighting, and a general sense that the world was experienced as an unsafe place. He recalled a life of restraint, fear, tentativeness, loss, and isolation. Harold found his relationship with his mother particularly confusing, as her behavior toward him was typically inconsistent. One moment, she would be telling him that he was her best friend, and the next, she would be humiliating him with insults about his looks and mannerisms. As a result, he both feared his mother and longed for her love, attention, and approval. As he progressed through life, every rebuff reawakened his fears of not being good enough and made him acutely aware of the loneliness and isolation he endured.

Though Harold's stories were painful for him to tell and for me to listen to, he began to report an improvement in his sexual functioning and enjoyment. Orgasm was becoming easier to achieve, and he was experiencing sex as increasingly pleasurable. This trend appeared to continue as our sessions progressed and our relationship deepened. I found Harold to be an interesting man, and I believe his perception of my curiosity and concern for his life was welcomed and appreciated.

Harold began to reach out to friends and family he had not communicated with for several years. He still enjoyed his solitary time but reported experiencing a newfound enjoyment in social interactions. He joined a hiking group and decided to try online dating. One afternoon, while picking up his dry cleaning, he began a conversation with a 31-year-old woman, Sami, who was working behind the counter at the local dry cleaner. Harold found Sami to be extremely attractive and friendly, and he began making frequent trips to the dry cleaner.

One day, Harold decided to ask Sami out for lunch. To his great surprise, she accepted. Harold was delighted and began looking forward to seeing Sami socially. Sami was a recently divorced mother of a young girl and had recently moved to New Jersey from Oregon. She knew few people in the area and was also a bit of a loner. She and Harold began seeing each other frequently, but the relationship remained platonic. Apparently, Sami saw Harold as a mentor and supportive friend. For his part, Harold had more romantic feelings toward Sami, but much as in his marriage, he did not crave partnered sex. Rather, he discovered a feeling of "aliveness" in his relationship with Sami, and he relished her appreciation of his cultural sophistication and her enthusiasm for accompanying him to museums, films, and concerts.

Harold reported a significantly enriched sexual enjoyment through masturbation as well as a generally enhanced overall life satisfaction. Harold's relationship with Sami flourished for approximately 8 months, after which Sami relocated back to the West Coast to be closer to her sister and her sister's family. While disappointed at not being able to see Sami regularly, Harold recognized that his relationship with Sami "brought him back to life" and provided him with a renewed sense of "meaning." Harold reported feeling like a "wet blanket" was lifted from covering him, and he found much greater enjoyment in his days. He felt much less lonely, and his fear of his own death substantially diminished. Harold and Sami maintained regular contact via FaceTime, and Harold continued to pursue limited social opportunities with verve. Sexually, Harold was also quite content.

Harold's case illustrates several seminal points of existential sex therapy. At 82 years old, Harold was still desirous of sexual pleasure. However, he was struggling with some of the existential aspects of aging and mortality. Harold experienced life as significant and meaningful during his long marriage to Jocelyn. Her presence enhanced his core, and the depth of their relationship helped mollify the pain and disappointment of having neither the childhood or the vocation he had desired. Harold spent much of his life as a loner who was deeply fearful and mistrusting of people. Sharing a life with Jocelyn, albeit not a sexual one, brought Harold out of his prison of solitude and provided him with the aliveness of interaction and intimate connection. Despite his anguish, when Jocelyn became ill, Harold basked in the pleasure of taking care of her. He was a doting husband and caretaker, and her eventual death left Harold feeling lost and alone. His penis, the great communicator, reflected his sad and isolated existence. He experienced both as "lifeless."

Therapy was extremely impactful for Harold. Our work, character-ized by my genuine interest in his life and my desire to establish an intimate, therapeutic connection with him, allowed for the building of a deep, connected, and emotionally meaningful relationship. Harold's case is a striking example of the power of the therapeutic relationship to heal. Recall earlier in this book, Yalom's exhortation that the therapeutic relationship is the therapist's most potent tool. Harold's strong feelings of connection with me allowed him to begin to take greater emotional risks outside of the consultation room and seek out opportunities for connec-tion with others. This led to his meeting Sami and the development of a warm and mutually nurturing connection. Beginning with the relation-ship that evolved between Harold and me, based on my fervent interest in learning about him and his life, he was able to risk connection with Sami and find renewed meaning and richness in life. His return to a life of vitality was reflected in the increased responsiveness of his penis and the rediscovery of his sexual pleasure.

Harold's case demonstrates that even in our elderly patients, the penis still speaks, although now it may whisper. Harold's loss of vitality and meaning was mirrored in the reduced sensation and animation of his penis. For Harold, being alive was expressed via the sensation (or lack thereof) emanating from his penis. His loss of penile sensitivity was his penis mirroring his feelings of isolation, loneliness, loss of meaning, and mortality. Connection with others was Harold's lifeblood, and the resto-ration and rejuvenation of his relational life was the key to his return to the land of the living.

Yalom (2008) reminds us that the antidote to much of human pain and anguish is connection with others. Connectedness and a deep rela-tional life can temper the despair of transiency. Of course, there are lim-its to the power of connection, and for many, the existential dread of mortality is also tied to feelings of not having lived a life that was worth-while and meaningful, having lived with significant regrets and refus-ing to accept the reality that everyone's existence will eventually fade. However, Yalom (2008) states with conviction that while human con-nection alone cannot eliminate our fears of death and being separated from the world around us, living a relational life greatly eases the sting of having to face the end. He recalls a patient, a woman dying, who shared in her thoughts in therapy group. She said:

> It's a pitch-black night. I'm alone in my boat floating in a harbor. I see the lights of many other boats. I know I can't reach them, can't join with them. But how comforting it is to see all those other lights bobbing in the harbor.
>
> (Yalom, 2008, p. 180)

While Yalom's patient accepted that she must die alone, the solace of connection to others and knowing there were those with whom she felt nurtured and loved accompanying her on this final journey brought her great comfort and succor. It is also noteworthy that both Harold and Ebenezer Scrooge found connection and meaning late in life. Many of our patients who have not lived well may feel that it is too late for them to redeem their lives. The stories of Harold and Ebenezer Scrooge demonstrate that it is never too late. As clinicians, we can help our patients find happiness and a rich relational life at any time. It is never too late, until it is.

I began this book with a story about my mother. I would like to conclude with one more. My mother was known for her "Life is good" philosophy and t-shirts. She died, unexpectedly, from a surgical accident one month shy of her 85th birthday. The night before her surgery, she and I were sitting in her living room, and she said to me, "Dan, tomorrow's procedure should be easy and uncomplicated. But just in case it doesn't go well, please don't be too sad. I have lived a wonderful life. I've done everything I've wanted, gotten more than I could have ever imagined, and loved the ride. I'm not ready to go, but if I have to, I have lived a wonderful life."

Thank you, Mom. I have missed you terribly, but your words that night were a beautiful gift and a deeply inspiring message. Life is good.

AND IN THE END...

In the end, I certainly hope you enjoyed this book. Men are more complicated, both psychologically and physically, than is often recognized. It is my hope that after reading this book, you will have a deeper appreciation for the psychological and sexual struggles of men as well as the highly nuanced messages that men often communicate. Of course, life would be easier if men were more adept at recognizing their emotional conflicts and expressing their distress verbally, but at least for now, we must learn the language of "penis-speak."

For so long, texts on male sexuality have focused on sexual performance and the distress many men experience if they are unable to have strong erections suitable for sexual intercourse. However, little consideration or exploration has been given to the meaning a functional or non-functional penis has for a man. This book has been an attempt to better understand the deeper significance of penile function and dysfunction and assist clinicians in better addressing the sexual and relational concerns of men.

DOI: 10.4324/9781003127871-9

This is a book about the psychological lives of men. Specifically, the *existential* psychological lives of men and how many of the psychological concerns of men are communicated through the functioning, or lack thereof, of their penis. A man's penis can be such a valuable messenger. A man's penis tells him when he is in the path of some perceived threat to his existence. Largely rooted in early childhood trauma that gets triggered in adulthood, a man's penis will self-protectively shut down to help him when his protective unconscious senses danger.

Similarly, when men behave in sexually inappropriate ways, it is not always rooted in the need for power, dominance, or hubris. Repressed feelings, particularly those resulting from trauma, will often burst through a man's defensive denial and manifest themselves with sexual indicators. Some situations will self-protectively result in a sexual shutdown (i.e., sexual dysfunction), while others may explode into uncharacteristic and unacceptable sexual comportment.

In this book, I have introduced you to several men who have struggled with their sexuality and the confusing and misunderstood messages sent via their penis. Recall the existential angst of returning war veterans, such as Ray, or the traumatic genital injury suffered by David, and the existential pain, as well as the anger expressed by Samuel following his prostate cancer surgery and the resulting sexual complications. They shared with us their feeling of living like "broken men" when their penile functioning was tragically altered. Remember the self-protective penile shutdowns of James, Edward, David, Herb, Martin, Ernie, Roger, Russ, and Ascher when early childhood trauma was triggered in their adult relationships, resulting in distressing sexual dysfunction. We also examined the futile attempts to keep traumatic memories repressed when presented with a trigger of mortality in the cases of Tim, Donald, Nicholas, Marcus, and Gustav and the problematic sexual behavior manifested by Franklin, Eric, Pete, and Carlos. Each of these men faced real or potential threats to their existence, to their mortality. In each of these cases, we see how oftentimes, especially in the face of traumatic change, sex, the vital life force, is called upon to counter the fears of death. It is these often-hidden wounds that must become more recognized by sex therapists if we are to assist men in dealing with their existential concerns and regain sexually satisfying lives.

Parkes (1975) recognizes that people are only open and receptive to new beliefs and behaviors once they have effectively processed and grieved for their loss of their assumptive world. I have tried to impress upon you throughout this book my belief that one of the primary reasons that the standard, behaviorally based interventions so common in traditional sex therapy approaches fail is because they move too quickly to push men to accept change without having spent the necessary time to help them understand, acknowledge, and process the ramifications of their loss of penile function. This is especially true for those whose penile functioning will not be restored, most notably our patients facing the effects of aging, illness, or injury, but this is also true of our male patients who are experiencing a loss of penile functioning due to the triggering of early trauma. The triggering of trauma also shatters a person's assumptive world and allows them the opportunity to finally revisit that trauma, understand it, and develop new ways of living with it.

Existential psychotherapy, particularly the teachings of Irvin Yalom, has suggested that we are relational beings. It is for this reason that I believe that existential psychotherapy has much to offer the sex therapy world. In most all his writings, Yalom reminds us of the importance of connection and the realization of our potential. If we can assist our patients in living meaningful, satisfying, and deeply connected relational lives, we will be doing humankind a great service. However, we, as clinicians, must be able to view human suffering through an existential lens. Yalom's four existential givens—meaning, freedom, isolation, and death—often underlie the triggering of male sexual dysfunction. An awareness and appreciation of these givens will assist sex therapists in getting to the roots of a man's sexual angst. Of course, you need not be an existential psychotherapist to find these psychotherapeutic tenets useful. An understanding of Yalom's principles can deepen and enrich whatever form of therapy you prefer to practice. Be it cognitive-behavioral, psychodynamic, emotionally focused, acceptance and commitment, systems, etc., Yalom's work and the adaptations of his work described in this book will hopefully make your practice of sex therapy and psychotherapy more meaningful for both you and your patients.

I mentioned in Chapter 2 that existential philosophy and existential psychotherapy are best suited for the curious. Well, my curiosity has been piqued by writing this book. There are so many questions about the penis, its messages, and its importance as a life force that remain unanswered. For example, I know so little about the inner world of transgender men. So much of what is written about the trans world has focused on the transition process, but so little of their experience of being male or female or their inner sexual lives has been understood. For example, what is the importance of the penis to someone who believes it to be foreign to their gender? How desirable is a penis to someone who believes their body was supposed to have one? What are the effects of gender-affirming surgery on one's perception of the penis? Does the surgical removal of a penis create a sense of loss, or does the gender correction carry such a sense of authenticity that the penis is little more than an unnecessary appendage that is best dispensed with? For those who have a surgically constructed penis, does this become an important addition to the affirmation of their genuine being? How about those who do not choose gender-affirming surgery? Do they wish they could either rid themselves of a penis or gain an important affirming symbol of maleness? There is so much to learn and so much that is yet unknown.

And what of those aging men we do not see in our practices? What is the significance of a quiet penis to them? Have they lived so well that death, as represented through an unresponsive penis, is not a concern? Do they long for sex or, as Schmid (2015) reminds us in Chapter 7, touch is what is most desired? Do men who have lived well accept the loss of sexual function and the decrease (or absence) of sexual activity as a natural, expected part of the life cycle?

A man's penis is fascinating, but we need to have a greater respect for its insight, wisdom, and messages.

Gentlemen, your penis speaks. Are you listening?

Appendix I

WORLD CONFEDERATION FOR EXISTENTIAL THERAPY STATEMENT ON THE NATURE OF EXISTENTIAL THERAPY

Existential therapy is a philosophically informed approach to counselling or psychotherapy. It comprises a richly diverse spectrum of theories and practices. Due partly to its evolving diversity, existential therapy is not easily defined. For instance, some existential therapists do not consider this approach to be a distinct and separate "school" of counselling or psychotherapy, but rather an attitude, orientation, or stance toward therapy in general. However, in recent years, existential therapy is increasingly considered by others to be a particular and specific approach unto itself. In either case, it can be said that though difficult to formalize and define, at its heart, existential therapy is a profoundly philosophical approach characterized in practice by an emphasis on relatedness, spontaneity, flexibility, and freedom from rigid doctrine or dogma. Indeed, due to these core qualities, to many existential therapists, the attempt to define it seems contradictory to its very nature.

As with other therapeutic approaches, existential therapy primarily (but not exclusively) concerns itself with people who are suffering and in crisis. Some existential therapists intervene in ways intended to alleviate or mitigate such distress when possible and assist individuals to contend with life's inevitable challenges in a more meaningful, fulfilling, authentic, and constructive manner. Other existential therapists are less symptom centered or problem -oriented and engage their clients in a wide-ranging exploration of existence without presupposing any particular therapeutic goals or outcomes geared toward correcting cognitions and behaviors, mitigating symptoms or remedying deficiencies. Nevertheless, despite their significant theoretical, ideological, and practical differences, existential therapists share a particular philosophically derived worldview that distinguishes them from most other contemporary practitioners.

Existential therapy generally consists of a supportive and collaborative exploration of patients' or clients' lives and experiences. It places primary importance on the nature and quality of the here-and-now therapeutic relationship, as well as on an exploration of the relationships between clients and their contextual lived worlds beyond the consulting room. In keeping with its strong philosophical foundation, existential therapy takes the human condition itself—in all its myriad facets, from tragic to wondrous, horrific to beautiful, material to spiritual—as its central focus. Furthermore, it considers all human experience as intrinsically inseparable from the ground of existence, or "being-in-the-world," in which we each constantly and inescapably participate.

Existential therapy aims to illuminate the way in which each unique person—within certain inevitable limits and constraining factors—comes to choose, create, and perpetuate his or her own way of being in the world. In both its theoretical orientation and practical approach, existential therapy emphasizes and honors the perpetually emerging, unfolding, and paradoxical nature of human experience and brings an unquenchable curiosity to what it truly means to be human. Ultimately, it can be said that existential therapy confronts some of the most fundamental and perennial questions regarding human existence: "Who am I?" "What is my purpose in life?" "Am I free or determined?" "How do I deal with my own mortality?" "Does my existence have any meaning or significance?" "How shall I live my life?"

Existential therapists see their practice as a mutual, collaborative, encouraging, and explorative dialogue between two struggling human beings—one of whom is seeking assistance from the other, who is professionally trained to provide it. Existential therapy places special emphasis on cultivating a caring, honest, supportive, empathic yet challenging relationship between therapist and client, recognizing the vital role of this relationship in the therapeutic process.

In practice, existential therapy explores how clients' here-and-now feelings, thoughts, and dynamic interactions within this relationship and with others might illuminate their wider world of past experiences, current events, and future expectations. This respectful, compassionate, supportive yet nonetheless very real encounter—coupled with a phenomenological stance—permits existential therapists to more accurately comprehend and descriptively address the person's way of being in the world. Taking great pains to avoid imposing their own worldview and value system upon clients or patients, existential therapists may seek to disclose and point out certain inconsistencies, contradictions or incongruence in someone's chosen but habitual ways of being . . . [The] therapeutic aim is to illuminate, clarify, and place these problems into a broader perspective so as to promote clients' capacity to recognize, accept, and actively exercise their responsibility and freedom: to choose how to be or act differently, if such change is so desired; or, if not, to tolerate, affirm, and embrace their chosen ways of being in the world.

Existential therapy does not define itself predominantly on the basis of any particular predetermined technique(s). Indeed, some existential therapists eschew the use of any technical interventions altogether, concerned that such contrived methods may diminish the essential human quality, integrity, and honesty of the therapeutic relationship. However, the one therapeutic practice common to virtually all existential work is the phenomenological method. Here, the therapist endeavors to be as fully present, engaged, and free of expectations as possible during each and every therapeutic encounter by attempting to temporarily put aside all preconceptions regarding the process. The purpose is to gain a clearer contextual in-depth understanding and acceptance of what a certain experience might signify to this specific person at this particular time in his or her life (Cooper et al., 2019).

BIBLIOGRAPHY

Agronin, M.E. (2014). Sexuality and aging. In Y.M. Binik & K.S.K. Hall (Eds.), *Principles and practice of sex therapy, 5th edition* (pp. 525–539). New York: Guilford Press.

Allen, W. (Director). (1986). *Hannah and her sisters* [Film]. Orion Pictures.

Allen, W. (Director). (2011). *Midnight in Paris* [Film]. Sony Pictures.

American Psychiatric Association. (2000). *Diagnostic and statistical manual of mental disorders, 4th edition, text revision.* Washington, DC: American Psychiatric Association Press.

American Psychiatric Association. (2013). *Diagnostic and statistical manual of mental disorders, 5th edition.* Washington, DC: American Psychiatric Association Press.

American Psychological Association. (2015). *Demographics of the U.S. psychology workforce: Findings from the American Community Survey.* Washington, DC: Author.

Atlas, G. (2022). *Emotional inheritance: A therapist, her patients, and the legacy of trauma.* New York: Little, Brown, Spark.

Barker, M. (2011). Existential sex therapy. *Sexual and Relationship Therapy,* 26, 33–47.

Barker, M. & Langdridge, D. (2013). The challenge of sexuality and embodiment in human relationships. In E. van Deurzen & S. Iacovou (Eds.), *Existential perspectives on relationship therapy.* New York: Palgrave Macmillan.

Becker, E. (1997). *The denial of death*. New York: Free Press.

Belcher, D. (2020, March 4). My father at 100, as seen from the age he died. *The New York Times*. Retrieved from: www.nytimes.com/2020/03/04/opinion/fathers-birthday-anniversary.html.

Berman, J. (2019). *Writing the talking cure: Irvin D. Yalom and the literature of psychotherapy*. Albany, NY: SUNY Press.

Berman, J. & Mosher, P.W. (2019). *Off the tracks: Cautionary tales about the derailing of mental health care, volume 1: Sexual and nonsexual boundary violations*. New York: International Psychoanalytic Books.

Betchen, S.J. & Davidson, H.L. (2018). *Master conflict theory: A new model for practicing couples and sex therapy*. New York: Routledge.

Bouman, W.P. & Kleinplatz, P.J. (2016). Introduction: Moving towards understanding greater diversity and fluidity of sexual expression in older people. In W.P. Bouman & P.J. Kleinplatz (Eds.), *Sexuality and ageing* (pp. 1–3). New York: Routledge.

Braun-Harvey, D. & Vigorito, M.A. (2015). *Treating out of control sexual behavior: Rethinking sex addiction*. New York: Springer.

Brotto, L.A. (2018). *Better sex through mindfulness: How women can cultivate desire*. Vancouver, British Columbia, Canada: Greystone Books.

Brown, M.J., Masho, S.W., Perera, R.A., Mezuk, B., & Cohen, S.A. (2015). Sex and sexual orientation disparities in adverse childhood experiences and early age at sexual debut in the United States: Results from a nationally representative sample. *Child Abuse and Neglect, 46*, 89–102.

Burger, A. (2018). *Witness: Lessons from Elie Wiesel's classroom*. New York: Mariner Publishing.

Cantor, J.M., Klein, C., Lykins, A., Rullo, J.E., Thaler, L., & Walling, B.R. (2013). A treatment-oriented typology of self-identified hypersexuality referrals. *Archives of Sexual Behavior, 42*, 883–893.

Carnes, P. (1994). *Contrary to love: Helping the sexual addict*. Center City, MN: Hazelden Publishing.

Carnes, P. (2001). *Out of the shadows: Understanding sexual addiction*. Center City, MN: Hazelden Publishing.

Cascalheira, B.A., McCormack, M., Portch, E., & Wignall, L. (2021). Changes in sexual fantasy and solitary sexual practice during social lockdown among your adults in the UK. *Sexual Medicine, 9*, 1–8.

Cassell, E.J. (2004). *The nature of suffering and the goals of medicine, 2nd edition*. New York: Oxford University Press.

Chase, D. (1999, January 10). *The Sopranos: The pilot* [Television broadcast]. HBO.

Cooper, M., Craig, E., & van Deurzen, E. (2019). Introduction: What is existential therapy? In E. van Deurzen, E. Craig, A. Langle, K.J. Schneider, D. Tantam, & S. du Plock (Eds.), *The Wiley world handbook of existential therapy* (pp. 1–27). Hoboken, NJ: Wiley Blackwell.

Courtois, F. & Gerard, M. (2020). Sexuality in men and women with spinal cord injury. In K.S.K. Hall & I.M. Binik (Eds.), *Principles and practice of sex therapy, 6th edition* (pp. 470–487). New York: Guilford Press.

Dickens, C.A. (1843). *A Christmas Carol.* London: Chapman & Hall.

Ehrenreich, B. (2018). *Natural causes: An epidemic of wellness, the certainly of dying, and killing ourselves to live longer.* New York: Twelve.

Ellin, A. (2011). The golden years, polished with surgery. *The New York Times.* Retrieved August 8, 2011 from: www.nytimes.com.

Erikson, E.H. (1963). *Childhood and society, 2nd edition.* New York: W.W. Norton and Company.

Farzan, A.N. (2019, November 7). A veteran wounded by an IED is "feeling whole" now after a breakthrough penis and scrotum transplant. *The Washington Post.* Retrieved from: www.washingtonpost.com/nation/2019/11/07/penis-scrotum-transplant-success-us-veteran-ied-afghanistan/.

Findlay, R. (2017). A narrative approach to sex therapy. In Z.D. Peterson (Ed.), *The Wiley handbook of sex therapy* (pp. 231–249). Malden, MA: John Wiley & Sons Ltd.

Ford, G.G., Ewing, J.J., Ford, A.M., Ferguson, N.L., & Sherman, W.Y. (2004). Death anxiety and sexual risk taking: Different manifestations of the process of defense. *Current Psychology, 23,* 147–160.

Frankl, V.E. (1952). The pleasure principle and sexual neurosis. *The International Journal of Sexology, 5,* 128–130.

Frankl, V.E. (1959). *Man's search for meaning, revised and expanded edition.* New York: Pocket Books.

Frankl, V.E. (1975). Paradoxical intention and dereflection. *Psychotherapy: Theory, Research & Practice, 12*(3), 226–237.

Grady, D. (2017, January 13). Study maps "uniquely devastating" genital injuries among troops. *The New York Times.* Retrieved from: www.nytimes.com/2017/01/13/health/genital-injuries-among-us-troops.html.

Grady, D. (2018, April 23). "Whole again": A vet maimed by and IED receives a transplanted penis. *The New York Times.* Retrieved from: www.nytimes.com/2018/04/23/health/soldier-penis-transplant-ied.html.

Grubbs, J.B., Hook, J.P., Griffin, B.J., Griffin, B.J., Cushman, M.S., Hook, J.N., & Penberthy, J.K. (2017). Treating hypersexuality. In Z.D. Peterson (Ed.), *The Wiley handbook of sex therapy* (pp. 231–249). Malden, MA: John Wiley & Sons Ltd.

Haig, M. (2020). *The midnight library.* New York: Penguin.

Hall, S.S. (2015, September 16). Feature: The man who wants to beat back aging. *Science.* Retrieved from: www.science.org/content/article/feature-man-who-wants-beat-back-aging.

Hayes, M. (2017, December 28). Like father, like son: For Nick Saban, there is no greater compliment. *Bleacher report.* Retrieved from: https://bleacherreport.com/articles/2750674-like-father-like-son-for-nick-saban-theres-no-greater-compliment.

Hemingway, E. (1926). *The sun also rises.* New York: Scribner.

Hemingway, E. (1964). *A moveable feast.* New York: Scribner.

Hill, F. (2019, January 17). What it's like to visit an existential therapist. *The Atlantic,* 1–23.

Hillis, S.D., Anda, R.F., Felitti, V.J., & Marchbanks, P.A. (2001). Adverse childhood experiences and sexual risk behaviors in women: A retrospective cohort study. *Family Planning Perspectives,* 33(5), 206–211.

Hollis, J. (1998). *The Eden project: In search of the magical other.* Toronto, Ontario, CA: Inner City Books.

Hughes, J. (2021, December 26). Did Larry King's obsession with death fuel his "indomitable" will to live? *The New York Times.* Retrieved from: www.nytimes/interactive/2021/12/22/magazine/larry-king-death.html.

Iasenza, S. (2020). *Transforming sexual narratives: A relational approach to sex therapy.* New York: Routledge.

Jewison, N. (Director). (1987). *Moonstruck.* Metro Golden Mayer.

Johnson, S. (2017). An emotionally focused approach to sex therapy. In Z.D. Peterson (Ed.), *The Wiley handbook of sex therapy* (pp. 250–265). Malden, MA: John Wiley & Sons Ltd.

Kaplan, A.H. & Abrams, M. (1958). Ejaculatory impotence. *The Journal of Urology,* 79(6), 964–968.

Kaplan, H.S. (1974). *The new sex therapy: Active treatment of sexual dysfunctions.* New York: Brunner/Mazel.

King, B. (2020). Average-size erect penis: Fiction, fact, and the need for counseling. *Journal of Sex and Marital Therapy,* 47(1), 80–89.

Kipnis, L. (2014). *Men: Notes from an ongoing investigation.* New York: Metropolitan Books.

Kleinplatz, P.J. (1998). Sex therapy for vaginismus: A review, critique, and humanistic alternative. *Journal of Humanistic Psychology*, 38(2), 51–81.

Kleinplatz, P.J. (2001). Introduction: A critical evaluation of sex therapy: Room for improvement. In P.J. Kleinplatz (Ed.), *New directions in sex therapy: Innovations and alternatives* (pp. xi–xxxiii). New York: Taylor & Francis.

Kleinplatz, P.J. (2003a). Beyond sexual mechanics and hydraulics: Humanizing the discourse surrounding erectile dysfunction. *Journal of Humanistic Psychology*, 43(10), 1–29.

Kleinplatz, P.J. (2003b). What's new in sex therapy: From stagnation to fragmentation. *Sexual and Relationship Therapy*, 18(1), 95–106.

Kleinplatz, P.J. (2010). Lessons from great lovers. In S. Levine, S. Althof, & C. Risen (Eds.), *The handbook of clinical sexuality for mental health professionals, 2nd edition* (pp. 57–72). New York: Routledge.

Kleinplatz, P.J. (2017). An existential-experiential approach to sex therapy. In Z.D. Peterson (Ed.), *The Wiley handbook of sex therapy* (pp. 218–230). Hoboken, NJ: Wiley Blackwell.

Kontula, O. & Haavio-Mannila, E. (2009). The impact of aging on human sexual activity and sexual desire. *Journal of Sex Research*, 46, 46–56.

Lantz, J. (1993). *Existential family therapy: Using the concepts of Viktor Frankl.* Northvale, NJ: Jason Aronson, Inc.

Lehrman, P.R. (1940). Freud's contributions to science. *Harofe Haivri (Hebrew Physician)*, 1, 161–176.

Leiblum S.R. & Sachs, J. (2002). *Getting the sex you want: A woman's guide to becoming proud, passionate, and pleased in bed.* New York: ASJA Press.

Levenson, J.S., Willis, G.M., & Prescott, D.S. (2017). *Trauma informed care: Transforming treatment for people who have sexually abused.* Brandon, VT: Safer Society Press.

Levine, S.B. (1988). *Sex is not simple.* Columbus, OH: Ohio Psychology Publishing Co.

Ley, D.J. (2014). *The myth of sexual addiction.* Lanham, MD: Rowman and Littlefield Publishing.

Lindau, S.T., Schumm, L.P., Laumann, E.O., Levinson, W., O'Muircheartaigh, C.A., & Waite, L.J. (2007). A study of sexuality and health among older adults in the United States. *New England Journal of Medicine*, 357, 762–774.

Masters, W.H. & Johnson, V.E. (1970). *Human sexual inadequacy.* Boston: Little, Brown, & Co.

Mate, G. (2011). *When the body says no: Exploring the stress-disease connection.* Hoboken, NJ: John Wiley & Sons.

May, R. (1953). *Man's search for himself.* New York: W.W. Norton & Company.

McCarthy, B. & McCarthy E. (2021). *Contemporary male sexuality: Confronting myths and promoting change.* New York: Routledge.

McCarthy, B.W. & Metz, M.E. (2007). *Men's sexual health: Fitness for satisfying sex.* New York: Routledge.

Meana, M., Hall, K.S.K., & Binik, Y.M. (2020). Conclusion: Where is sex therapy going? In K.S.K. Hall & Y.M. Binik (Eds.), *Principles and practice of sex therapy, 6th edition* (pp. 505–522). New York: Guilford Press.

Menard, A.D., Kleinplatz, P.J., Rosen, L., Lawless, S., Paradis, N., Campbell, M., & Huber, J.D. (2016). Individual and relational contributors to optimal sexual experiences in older men and women. In W.P. Bouman & P.J. Kleinplatz (Eds.), *Sexuality and ageing* (pp. 78–93). New York: Routledge.

Mental Health Worker. (2021, September 9). Mental health professional statistics and facts in the U.S. *Mental health worker.* Retrieved from: www. zippia.com/mental-health-professional-jobs/demographics/.

Merrick, M.T., Ports, K.A., Ford, D.C., Afifi, T.O., Gershoff, E.T., & Grogan-Kaylor, A. (2017). Unpacking the impact of adverse childhood experience on adult mental health. *Childhood Abuse & Neglect*, 69, 10–19.

Metz, M.E. & McCarthy, B.W. (2007). The "good-enough sex" model for men's and couples' satisfaction. *Sexual and Relationship Therapy*, 22, 351–362.

Mickey Mantle Quotes. Archived from the original on October 13, 2011. Retrieved May 2, 2020 from: Baseball-almanac.com.

Miller, A. (1981). *The drama of the gifted child: The search for the true self.* New York: Basic Books.

Miller, M. (2021, December). One pill makes you . . . immortal? *Outside.* Retrieved from: https://apple.news/AOmxPGRRcRuCk4g0XCARm5A.

Miller, R.L. & Mulligan, R.D. (2002). Terror management: The effects of mortality salience and locus of control on risk-taking behaviors. *Personality and Individual Differences*, 33(7), 1203–1214.

Mintz, L. (2017). *Becoming cliterate: Why orgasm equality matters—and how to get it.* New York: HarperOne.

Miranda, L-M. (2015). *Non-Stop: On Hamilton.* Atlantic.

Mitchell, R. (Director). (1999). *Notting Hill.* Universal Pictures.

Moser, C. (2011). Hypersexual disorder: Just more muddled thinking. *Archives of Sexual Behavior*, 40, 227–229.

Murtagh, J. (1989). The "small" penis syndrome. *Australian Family Physician*, 18, 20.

Nelson, T. (2020). Sex and imago relationship therapy. In T. Nelson (Ed.), *Integrative sex and couples therapy: A therapist's guide to new and innovative approaches* (pp. 45–58). Eau Claire, WI: PESI Publishing and Media.

The New York Times. (2022, July 5). Covid in the U.S: Latest map and case count. *The New York Times*. Retrieved from: www.nytimes.com/interactive/2020/us/coronavirus-us-cases.html.

Newell, A.G. (1978). A case of ejaculatory incompetence treated with a mechanical aid. In J. LoPiccolo & L. LoPiccolo (Eds.), *The handbook of sex therapy: Perspectives in sexuality (behavior, research, and therapy)* (pp. 291–293). Boston, MA: Springer.

Nuland, S.B. (1993). *How we die: Reflections on life's final chapter.* New York: Vintage Books.

Ofri, D. (2019). A brush. *Ascent.* Retrieved from: https://readthebesetwriting.com/a-brush-danielle/ofri/.

Parkes, C.M. (1975). What become of redundant world models? A contribution to the study of adaptation to change. *British Journal of Medical Psychology*, 48, 131–137.

Pastoor, H. & Gregory, A. (2020). Penile size dissatisfaction. *Journal of Sexual Medicine*, 17, 1400–1404.

Perel, E. (2017). *The state of affairs: Rethinking infidelity.* New York: HarperCollins.

Perelman, M.A. & Watter, D.N. (2014). Delayed ejaculation. In P.S. Kirana, M.F. Tripodi, Y. Reisman, & H. Porst (Eds.), *The EFS and ESSM syllabus of clinical sexology* (pp. 660–672). Amsterdam: Medix Publishers.

Perelman, M.A. & Watter, D.N. (2016). Delayed ejaculation. In S.B. Levine, C.B. Risen, & S.E. Althof (Eds.), *The handbook for clinical sexuality for mental health professionals, 3rd edition.* New York: Routledge.

Prescott, D.S., Plummer, C., & Davis, G. (2010). Recognition, response, and resolution: Historical responses to rape and child molestation. In K.L. Kaufman (Ed.), *The prevention of sexual violence: A practitioner's sourcebook.* Holyoke, MA: NEARI Press.

Pyke, R.E. (2020). Sexual performance anxiety. *Sexual Medicine Reviews*, 8(2), 183–190.

Roberts, R. & Smith, J. (2018). *A season in the sun: The rise of Mickey Mantle*. New York: Basic Books.

Rosenbaum, B. (1987, April). Life with Rod: A conversation with Carol Serling. *Twilight Zone Magazine*. Retrieved from: www.bobrosenbaum.com.

Roth, P. (1967). *Portnoy's complaint*. New York: Vintage Books.

Roth, P. (2001). *The dying animal*. New York: Vintage Books.

Routledge, C. (2018, June 23). Suicides have increased: Is this an existential crisis? *The New York Times*. Retrieved from: www.nytimes.com/2018/06/23/opinion/sunday/suicide-ra . . . =opinion-c-col-right-region&WT.nav=opinion-c-col-right-region.

Sagar, P. (2018). On going on and on and on. *AEON*. Retrieved September 5, 2018 from: https://aeon.com/essays/theres-a-big-problem-with-immortality-it-goes-on-and-on.

Sale, A. (2021). *Let's talk about hard things*. New York: Simon & Schuster.

Schaumburg, H. (1997). *False intimacy: Understanding the struggle of sexual addiction*. Colorado Springs, CO: NavPress.

Schmid, S. (2015). *What we gain as we grow older*. New York: Upper West Side Philosophers, Inc.

Schover, L.R. (1984). *Prime time: Sexual health for men over fifty*. New York: Holt, Rinehart, and Winston Publishing.

Schover, L.R. & Leiblum, S.R. (1994). Commentary: The stagnation of sex therapy. *Journal of Psychology and Human Sexuality*, 6(3), 5–30.

Shakespeare, W. & Muir, K. (1999). *Richard II: Signet classics, 2nd revised edition*. New York: Signet.

Shaw, J. (2001). Approaching sexual potential in relationship: A reward of age and maturity. In P.J. Kleinplatz (Ed.), *New directions in sex therapy: Innovations and alternatives* (pp. 185–209). New York: Brunner-Routledge.

Sifferlin, A. (2018). Is an anti-aging pill on the horizon? *Time Magazine*. Retrieved from: http://time.com/5159879/is-an-anti-aging-pill-on-the-horizon/?utm_source=time.come&utm_medium=email&utm_campaign=social=button-sharing.

Solomon, S. (2019). Grave matters: On the role of death in life. *Independent Practitioner*, Fall, 14–16.

Spinelli, E. (1997). *Tales of un-knowing: Eight stories of existential therapy*. New York: New York University Press.

Spitz, A. (2018). *The penis book*. Emmaus, PA: Rodale Press.

Stadlen, N. (2013). The challenge of intimacy: Fear of the other. In E. van Deurzen & S. Iacovou (Eds.), *Existential perspectives on relationship therapy*. New York: Palgrave Macmillan.

Stulhoffer, A., Hinchliff, S., Jurin, T., Hald, G.M., & Traeen, B. (2018). Successful aging and changes in sexual interest and enjoyment among older European men and women. *Journal of Sexual Medicine*, 15, 1393–1402.

Szasz, T. (1980). *Sex by prescription*. New York: Penguin Books.

Taddeo, L. (2019). *Three women*. New York: Avid Reader Press.

Theobald, S. (2020, November 2). How is Betty Dodson, the queen of female masturbation, dying? Not quietly. *The Daily Beast*. Retrieved from: https://thedailybeast.com/how-is-betty-dodson-the-queen-of-female-masturbation-dying-not-quietly?ref=home.

Thomas, D. (1957). *The collected poems of Dylan Thomas*. New York: New Directions Publishing.

Thurber, J. & White, E.B. (1929). *Is sex necessary?* New York: Harper.

University of Michigan. (2018). Let's talk about sex. *National poll on healthy aging*. retrieved October 10, 2018 from: www.healthyagingpoll.org/report/let's-talk-about-sex.

Van Der Kolk, B. (2014). *The body keeps the score: Brain, mind, and body in the healing of trauma*. New York: Penguin Books.

Van Deurzen, E. (2013). The challenge of human relations and relationship therapy: To live and to love. In E. van Deurzen & S. Iacovou (Eds.), *Existential perspectives on relationship therapy*. New York: Palgrave Macmillan.

Van Deurzen, E. & Iacovou, S. (2013a). A developing model of existential relationship therapy. In E. van Deurzen & S. Iacovou (Eds.), *Existential perspectives on relationship therapy*. New York: Palgrave Macmillan.

Van Deurzen, E. & Iacovou, S. (2013b). Introduction: Setting the scene: Relatedness from an existential perspective. In E. van Deurzen & S. Iacovou (Eds.), *Existential perspectives on relationship therapy*. New York: Palgrave Macmillan.

Viscott, D. (1996). *Emotional resilience: Simple truths for dealing with the unfinished business of your past*. New York: PenguinRandomHouse.

Wainwright III, L. (2012). Older than my old man now [Recorded by Louden Wainright III]. On the album *Older than my old man now*. StorySound Records.

Watter, D.N. (1994). *Widower's syndrome: Sexual dysfunction following the death of a spouse*. Presentation to the New Jersey Association of Cognitive-Behavioral Therapists, Westfield, New Jersey, May 22nd.

Watter, D.N. (1998). Erectile dysfunction in widowed men: A somatic expression of grief. *The New Jersey Psychologist*, Spring, 23–25.

Watter, D.N. (2012). The medicalization of sex therapy: Better living through chemistry? *Journal of Ethics in Mental Health*, 7, 1–4.

Watter, D.N. (2018). Existential issues in sexual medicine: The relation between death anxiety and hypersexuality. *Sexual Medicine Reviews*, 6(3), 3–10.

Watter, D.N. (2020). Sexuality and aging: Navigating the sexual challenges of aging bodies. In K.S.K. Hall & Y.M. Binik (Eds.), *Principles and practice of sex therapy, 6th edition*. New York: Guilford Press.

Waxman, S. (2008). *Sex and death*. Los Angeles, CA: First Run Press.

Weeks, G.R., Gambescia, N., & Hertlein, K.M. (2016). *A clinician's guide to systematic sex therapy, 2nd edition*. New York: Routledge.

Weiner, L. & Avery-Clark, C. (2017). *Sensate focus in sex therapy: The illustrated manual*. New York: Routledge.

Wiesel, E. (1958). *Night*. New York: Hill and Wang.

Willingham, E. (2020). *Phallacy: Life lessons from the animal penis*. New York: Avery.

Wylie, K.R. & Eardley, I. (2007). Penile size and the "small penis syndrome". *British Journal of Urology*, 99, 1449–1455.

Yalom, I.D. (1980). *Existential psychotherapy*. New York: Basic Books.

Yalom, I.D. (1989). *Love's executioner & other tales of psychotherapy*. New York: Basic Books.

Yalom, I.D. (1992). *When Nietzsche wept*. New York: HarperCollins.

Yalom, I.D. (1996). *Lying on the couch*. New York: Basic Books.

Yalom, I.D. (1999). *Momma and the meaning of life*. New York: HarperCollins.

Yalom, I.D. (2002a). *The gift of therapy: An open letter to a new generation of therapists and their patients*. New York: HarperCollins.

Yalom, I.D. (2002b). Religion and psychiatry. *American Journal of Psychotherapy*, 56, 301–316.

Yalom, I.D. (2005). *The Schopenhauer cure*. New York: HarperCollins.

Yalom, I.D. (2008). *Staring at the sun: Overcoming the terror of death*. San Francisco, CA: Jossey-Bass.

Yalom, I.D. (2012). *The Spinoza problem*. New York: Basic Books.

Yalom, I.D. (2015). *Creatures of a day: And other tales of psychotherapy*. New York: Basic Books.

Yalom, I.D. (2017). *Becoming myself: A psychiatrist's memoir*. New York: Basic Books.

Yalom, I.D. & Leszcz, M. (2020). *The theory and practice of group therapy, 6th edition*. New York: Basic Books.

Yalom, I.D. & Yalom, M. (2021). *A matter of death and life*. Stanford, CA: Redwood Press.

Yeager, C. (1985). *Yeager: An autobiography*. New York: Bantam Books.

Zilbergeld, B. (1978). *Male sexuality*. New York: Bantam Books.

ABOUT DR. DANIEL N. WATTER

Dr. Daniel N. Watter received his doctoral degree from New York University in 1985 and has also earned a postgraduate certificate in medical humanities (with a concentration in medical ethics) from Drew University. He is licensed as both a psychologist and a marital and family therapist. In addition, he is board certified in sex therapy by the American Association of Sexuality Educators, Counselors, and Therapists (AASECT) and the American Board of Sexology (ACS), in which he also holds fellowship status. Dr. Watter is an AASECT-certified sex therapy supervisor and has been elected to fellowship status in the International Society for the Study of Women's Sexual Health (ISSWSH) and the Sexual Medicine Society of North America (SMSNA).

In addition to his clinical practice, Dr. Watter has held several faculty appointments. Currently, he is a faculty member at the University of Michigan School of Social Work's sexual certification program and the Modern Sex Therapy Institutes. He has served as an adjunct professor of psychology at Fairleigh Dickinson, Drew, and Seton Hall Universities, a clinical instructor of OB/GYN and Women's Health at University of Medicine and Dentistry of New Jersey-New Jersey Medical School, and a clinical assistant professor of psychiatry and behavioral medicine at the New York College of Osteopathic Medicine. Dr. Watter is also a former member of the medical staff of the Saint Barnabas Medical Center in Livingston, New Jersey, and served on the Medical Center's ethics committee.

Dr. Watter is a member of several professional organizations and has been elected to leadership positions in many. He has completed two terms on the New Jersey Psychological Association's ethics committee, where he spent two years as the committee's chairperson. He has also served two terms as the secretary/treasurer of the Society for Sex Therapy and Research (SSTAR), where he previously served as membership officer. Dr. Watter is also the former chair of the diplomate certification committee for the American Association for Sexuality Educators, Counselors, and Therapists (AASECT). From 2019 to 2021, he was the chair of the AASECT ethics advisory committee. In addition, he is a past president of SSTAR. In 2009, Dr. Watter was appointed by New Jersey's governor to the State Board of Psychological Examiners. He was reappointed in 2017.

A frequent lecturer at professional meetings throughout North America, Dr. Watter is the author of more than 30 professional articles and book chapters on topics such as sexual function and dysfunction and ethics in healthcare practice.

INDEX

For Product Safety Concerns and Information please contact our EU
representative GPSR@taylorandfrancis.com
Taylor & Francis Verlag GmbH, Kaufingerstraße 24, 80331 München, Germany

www.ingramcontent.com/pod-product-compliance
Lightning Source LLC
Chambersburg PA
CBHW071414290326
41932CB00047B/2902

*9 7 8 0 3 6 7 6 5 1 1 1 4 *